THE
RUTHLESS
LEADER

Other Books by Alistair McAlpine

THE RUTHLESS LEADER

THREE CLASSICS OF STRATEGY AND POWER

Edited by

Alistair McAlpine

JOHN WILEY & SONS, INC.

New York • Chichester • Weinheim • Brisbane • Singapore • Toronto

Published by John Wiley & Sons, Inc.
Published simultaneously in Canada.

Library of Congress Cataloging-in-Publication Data:

ISBN 0-471-37247-1

Printed in the United States of America.

10   9   8   7   6   5   4   3   2   1

Contents

v

THE
RUTHLESS
LEADER

Introduction

To demonstrate both his military might and will, Sun Tzu, a Chinese general who lived and wrote *The Art of War* some 2,500 years ago, set out to drill 180 ladies from the court of Prince He Lu. The exercise was a disaster, the ladies gossiped and dithered, always misunderstanding Sun Tzu's instructions. The great general, asserting that it was the responsibility of those in authority to convey instructions in such a way that those instructed would understand, explained to the ladies what he wanted them to do on each command in a way that could not possibly be misunderstood. The general then called for executioners to stand by to prove that he regarded discipline as the essence of military behavior. The drums beat, the commands were called, and the women this time stood still. Their giggles, however occasional, soon degenerating into raucous laughter. Once again, Sun Tzu told the ladies that commands incapable of comprehension are the fault of the commander and he repeated the drill. Again, the drums beat, the orders were called and once more the women laughed. Orders that are vague, Sun Tzu asserted, are the fault of the commanders. Orders that are clear, however, and still disobeyed are the fault of those commanded. With these remarks, the general ordered the

1

executioners to behead the two leading concubines, despite the protest of Prince He Lu. Sun Tzu then casually appointed two other women to lead the troop and proceeded with the drill. He knew the importance of discipline in warfare and he acted with utter ruthlessness to ensure that he had discipline even amongst these most unlikely of troops. The next time that the orders were called, the ladies drilled impeccably. As for the prince, he was called to witness this improbable sight, an offer that he declined out of anger at losing his favorite concubines. As a result, Prince He Lu earned Sun Tzu's contempt.

Whether this story is apocryphal does not really matter; it illustrates a principle—discipline—that is common to all three works in this volume: Sun Tzu's *The Art of War,* Nicolo Machiavelli's *The Prince* and my own *The Servant.* A disciplined approach to the task at hand, whether it be government, the serving of a prince, or the fighting of a war, is of the highest importance and nothing must be spared to achieve that end. Machiavelli in another of his books also entitled *The Art of War* spends a considerable number of words pointing out the need for discipline. Discipline via fear is, however, useful only up to a point. There also must be a motivating force for all people who aspire to succeed, whether in the field of business, politics, the arts, government, or warfare. This force of self-motivation is a deeper instinct than the impulses that lead to a lack of discipline or those that induce an irrational obsession with discipline. The discipline portrayed in *The Prince, The Servant,* and *The Art of War* is in a sense self-serving, for to act on self-motivation will undoubtedly produce a sense of self-satisfaction, the gratification of having truly tried to achieve an end.

The psychological motivations for power and discipline are explored in each of the three works. Sun Tzu's *The Art of War,* ostensibly about the tactics and the day-to-day practice of warfare, also bears a totally different interpretation: the tactics of day-to-day business. Because Sun Tzu was a keen observer of human nature, *The Art of War* is filled with advice useful not only for those engaged in war but also for those carrying on their normal lives. For Sun Tzu, war is war and the conduct of it is not to be obstructed by the whims of princes. If the cost of directing Prince He Lu's attention to Sun Tzu's military genius was the lives of a few concubines, then Sun Tzu did not hesitate to extract that price. Sun Tzu was ruthless in achieving his goal.

Likewise, in Machiavelli's *The Prince,* politics is war and any deceit, any chicanery, is possible. According to this principle, victory must be ruthlessly sought; the ends, no matter how treacherous, justify the means. As the following passage proves, "How honourable it is for a prince to keep his word, and act rather with integrity than collusion, I suppose everybody understands: nevertheless, experience has shown in our times that those princes who have not pinned themselves up to that punctuality and preciseness have done great things, and by their cunning and subtilty not only circumvented, and darted the brains of those with whom they had to deal, but have overcome and been too hard for those who have been so superstitiously exact." The means recommended by Machiavelli, however, are not always in the interest of the state. In his book "discourses," many of the most unscrupulous and cruel devices are to be used by citizens wanting to seize the government of the state.

In *The Servant,* the attendant must believe in the idea—a philosophy, developed by the Prince as leader by which he or she intends to rule the state. Nothing must stand in the way of the idea; if subtlety fails, then the ruthless approach must prevail. On behalf of the Prince, the servant acts out a series of comparatively minor but highly significant rules that need to be followed to beat all opponents. The servant, like the Prince and the military leader, is self-motivated and serves the Prince out of loyalty to the idea rather than loyalty to the Prince himself for this arrangement also serves the servants own self-interest.

The combination of these three works makes a devastating statement about human nature. In all, they contain advice to a Prince, counsel to the servant, suggestions that the servant gives to the Prince to achieve the servant's own end and instruction on how to keep the idea from erosion by the pressure of day-to-day political necessities of government. For *The Prince*, in the process of governing, will meet with a series of obstacles, each providing a temptation to deviate from the ideas. These texts comment on how human nature responds to an ideal, detailing an aspect of the nature that humans prefer to pretend does not exist, namely ruthlessness. These three works are ruthless, without a doubt. Today we might be tempted to mitigate their ruthless quality with the use of the word *pragmatic,* or perhaps we might prefer to pretend that such a ruthless approach is not for us. As long ago as the sixteenth century, Sir Francis Bacon corroborated the interpretation that Machiavelli's *The Prince* is hard-hearted when Bacon wrote in his work, *Advancement of Learning,* that, "We are much beholden to Machiavelli and others that write what men do and not what they ought to do." There is, however, despite their overt ruthless qualities, a strong view of subtlety in all three of these works. This subtlety is perhaps best expressed in the line by Sun Tzu, "Fighting to win one hundred victories in one hundred battles is not the supreme skill. However, to break the enemies' resistance without fighting is the supreme skill."

Critics of Machiavelli have led us to believe that his work is without principle. T. B. Macauly wrote, "Out of his surname they have coined an epithet for a knave and out of his Christian name a synonym for the devil." *The Prince* was treated as a cruel joke by Machiavelli's contemporaries, attacked by the Renaissance church, satirized by Elizabethan dramatists, studied by Richelieu and Napoleon—yet it also received the highest praise. People across the centuries have argued about the value of *The Prince* as a guide to living. Machiavelli claimed to have studied the ancients and used their actions and reactions to justify the conclusions in the book.

It can, however, be argued that Machiavelli, like Sun Tzu, studied those around him, discovering human instincts and describing his findings with telling truthfulness. The actions of the ancients, perhaps, merely providing justification for his hypotheses. I have reflected on *The Prince* for many years, concluding that, far from just providing advice to a Prince, Machiavelli has identified remarkable truths about the human character. *The Prince* is merely flesh around the skeleton of those truths. Nowhere in the entirety of *The Prince* does Machiavelli predict the downfall of a state or a ruler or, for that matter, even a contemporary general. Unlike Nostradamus and many others who predict dire events, even the demise of the world, Machiavelli confines himself entirely to an understanding of the circumstances of humankind. People, he demonstrates, come in all shapes and sizes and so it is with their natural intelligence. Machiavelli understood this and he also understood how people behave in the myriad of different circumstances in which they find themselves. He was, like all of us, a fallible human being beset with conceit, pride, and all the other aspects of our diverse characters.

To counter such fallibility, humankind has principles by which to live. These principles are also featured in *The Prince,* particularly in the last chapter entitled "An Exhortation to

Liberate Italy from the Barbarians." In his text, Machiavelli having already written a spirited attack on the temporal power of the Pope in the chapter "Of Ecclesiastical Principalities" by featuring the barbarians as Italy's enemies and including with them the Papal states, he reinforces this attack. Machiavelli is forthright in his desire to have a new Prince who would free Italy from her oppressor. Ruthlessness was, in this context, a last resort. "Poor Italy left half dead, expecting who would be her Samaritan to bind up her wounds, put an end of the sackings and devastations in Lombardy, the taxes and expilations in the kingdom of Naples and Tuscany, and cure her sores which length of time had festered and imposthumated." This exhortation is in the one idealistic chapter in the whole work; it stands alone in the passion of its writing. But is it an afterthought, or is it a carefully planned counterpoint to the rest of the work? Machiavelli here argues for casting out corruption and replacing the old order with a clean, idealistic, and principled new order. He calls on Italians to recapture their own land, and in the middle of the chapter he wrote a sentence that resonates to this day, "You have justice on your side; for that war is just which is necessary, and it is piety to fight where no hope is left in anything else." The nature of a *just* war taken from medieval warfare and allied to the order and discipline of the Renaissance was—and still is—a powerful concept. It is a concept that, however powerful, must surely be wrongheaded. Machiavelli then invokes the spirits of Moses, Cyrus, and Thesus along with the parting of the Red Sea and a bundle of other miracles as he calls on the magnificent Lorenzo Di Piero de' Medici to take up the sword to free Italy from its oppressors and the corruption of the old order. He must have touched a chord with Lorenzo when he wrote the words:

Nor is it any wonder if none of the aforenamed Italians have been able to do that which may be hoped for from your illustrious family; and if in so many revolutions in Italy, and so long continuation of war, their military virtue seems spent and extinguished, the reason is, their old discipline was not good, and nobody was able to direct a better. Nothing makes so much to the honor of a new prince as new laws and new orders invented by him, which, if they be well founded, and carry anything of grandeur along with them, do render him venerable and wonderful; and Italy is susceptible enough of any new form.

Despite the tour de force of the last chapter, Machiavelli did not receive the employment he sought, and his greatest work was not published until fifteen years after his death. The last chapter may well have been principled, but even Machiavelli saw a man rising to power by his methods as unlikely to have much virtue left by the time he attains his end. His assertion that men have evil in them as well as good is important when considering the ability of humankind to achieve something good and even great. In the last chapter of *The Prince,* Machiavelli envisions a self-made prince who will carry out the task of rejoining Italy. This seemingly impossible task can be carried out by no one except that self-made man, Guiliano de' Medici, to whom Machiavelli was offering the task as a destiny. The last chapter of *The Prince* is one about the goodness of opportunity—seizing the occasion to put something right, to make a person, place, or thing better.

Sun Tzu captures something of the sense of Machiavelli's last chapter when he stresses the importance of a positive attitude: "One who foresees victory before a battle will most probably win. One who predicts not much of a chance of winning before the fight, will most probably not win." If one does not believe in opportunity, how can one possibly recognize opportunity when it presents itself? In *The Art of War,* principle is also to be found in the unashamed act of winning. "Without harmony in the state no military expedition can be made. Without harmony in the army, no battle formation can be directed. In war, the general first receives his commands from the ruler. He then assembles his troops and blends them into a harmonious entity before pitching camp." The general fights in the interest of the state, and his army, a part of the state, fights with him. Once the ruler has given instructions, that is the end of the ruler's authority—as Sun Tzu demonstrated so dramatically when he allegedly cut off the heads of Prince He Lu's favorite concubines. "If the situation offers victory, but the ruler forbids fighting, the general may still fight. If the situation is such that he cannot win, then the general must not fight even if the ruler orders him to do so." The general's casual disregard for discipline seems at odds with Sun Tzu's earlier demonstrations of the consequences of such disobedience. The general, however, has a higher principle, or *idea,* in mind, one that overrides the mere views of a prince on whether to engage in battle or not. "Thus the general, who advances without coveting fame and withdraws without fearing disgrace, but whose sole intention is to protect the people and do good service for his ruler is the precious jewel of the state."

Here, Sun Tzu touches upon the hub of the relationship between the state, its prince, its servants, the citizens, and the idea. A state is run for the benefit of those people who make up that state. The idea should dominate that state's dealings with other states and the dealings of princes, generals, and officials with the citizens of that state. This principle is accepted by Machiavelli in *The Prince* where he argues that there is no more formidable a military force than that of citizens protecting their own state. It is the guiding principle in *The Servant,* in all his or her dealings, to protect the idea that is at one with the state and it's citizens. This principle also comes across quite clearly in *The Art of War.* "Such a general who protects his soldiers like infants will have them following him into the deepest valleys. A general who treats his soldiers like his own beloved sons will have their willingness to die with him." This is a demonstration of the ideal state in which the idea is unanimous with the motivations of the leaders, their "servants," and the society at large.

Seldom, however, has the population of aggressor states benefited in the long term from the ambitions of their leaders. As the Roman Empire fell, so did the empires that followed. As Machiavelli points out, military might is right, but only for the protection of your own territory. Even in the fifteenth century there was an awareness of the problem of ruling conquered territory. All three works in this volume advocate a state that serves its people and a people who serve their state. In all matters pertaining to warfare, *The Prince, The Servant,* and *The Art of War* agree that mercenaries are of little use in comparison to the forces raised within a state. Equally, they agree that for a prosperous state to live for any length of time at peace is unlikely; so in the same way that a prudent man arranges for the securing of his property, so a perceptive prince, servant, or general must make preparations for war to ensure peace. Princes and governments who plunder their own states come to a sticky end. *The Servant* is a work that is devoted to the actions necessary to ensure that the principle or the idea survive. Both the prince and the servant are in effect temporary guardians of the principle or the idea, for it, unlike them, knows no mortality. The idea must be preserved and protected by all means available. Warfare then is fundamentally attached to the idea; the prince, the general, the army, and the people at large may have to die in the act of protecting it. The concubines who learned military drill under

Sun Tzu's instructions learned that lesson. They, through folly, became a sacrifice for what was considered a greater good—the threat of death administered by one's own side is not, however, a valid method of motivating troops.

The notion that soldiers will fight fiercely on instruction, for any cause, is invalid. Self-motivation is vital. To fight fiercely, soldiers must believe in the idea as their leaders do. An idea that does not benefit one's family and friends and one's fellow soldiers and their friends and families is unlikely to inspire the best results in battle. Old soldiers admit that they fight not for grand ideals, but for the comrade who stands next to them. The ideas of a general benefit from victory, and general misery from defeat is an extension from this principle. A camaraderie or social well-being is the principle or idea by which soldiers are motivated. *The Art of War* and *The Prince* are both pragmatic works based on the premise that self-motivation moves people to take action that they might not otherwise have the courage to take. If the paramount motivating force is self-interest, then there can be no conflict regarding the idea motivating the people of a nation. After all, those who support the idea are self-interested. Their interest in the idea, however, unites them in a way that the self-interest of an individual never can.

Machiavelli and Sun Tzu each in his own stratagem are clearly convinced that national unity from which discipline flows is necessary to motivate a population into a fighting force. This idea can bring about a variety of effects, for instance, the desire to remove foreign troops from one's native soil or the desire to prevent one's nation from being consumed into a federation of neighboring states in a periodical rearrangement of a continent's boundaries. In this case, the idea is patriotism combined with nationalism, but it could have been about religion or different styles of government. Without the motivating force of the idea, all is lost—the nations, their institutions, and their people. In Machiavelli's final, emotional chapter of *The Prince,* Italians in peacetime are decadent and easy prey for any who would plunder their land. In wartime, they are beaten and oppressed and their land is plundered for the benefit of conquerors. Machiavelli's *idea* is the perfect prince. "It is manifest how she prays to God daily to send some person who may redeem her from the cruelty and insolence of the barbarians. It is manifest how prone and ready she is to follow the banner that any man will take up."

Machiavelli was, if nothing else, a politician. His ambivalent attitude to a unified Italy demonstrates this with considerable clarity. On one hand, he wrote that impassioned last chapter in *The Prince* calling for a unified Italy; and on the other hand, he was prepared to work for a Florentine government kept in power by France. Machiavelli, a Florentine by birth and instinct, was understandably suspicious of the Venetians. However, his chief accusation against them—the allegation that they were trying to unite Italy—was perverse. In our age, the inconsistencies of Machiavelli's character do not matter, for he understood politics; and after the publication of *The Prince,* politics changed in such a way that they would never be the same again. For the first time, humankind, or at least that part of it that read and thought, was prepared to admit the advancing of behavior that were generally accepted as evil. Machiavelli clearly enjoyed politics; every page of *The Prince* is packed with the enthusiasm and pleasure that he took in committing his knowledge to paper.

Machiavelli's ideas appeared original, but not because they had not been thought of before. Indeed, many cunning and successful men and women must surely have taken into account human failings when planning the downfall of their enemies.

Machiavelli's fame comes from the fact that he dared publish a work pointing out the inherent defects in the character of humankind. It is difficult to realize that a person may not behave with either morality, charity, or honor just because that is how one would like to believe that oneself would behave under similar circumstances. It is also important to understand that there are circumstances, albeit extreme circumstances, in which one would also behave without morality, charity, or honor. Most people, however, are reluctant to admit that this is true. This reality was demonstrated when President Clinton clearly behaved without morality, charity, or honor; yet despite overwhelming evidence, the American people refused to believe that this was the case. After all, in five years of his presidency, 25 million American jobs had been created and prosperity was the norm. The public did not wish to rock the boat.

As true today as when Machiavelli first presented the notion, the evil in humankind can be recognized for what it is and used to the advantage of one who is able to recognize it. Nearly five hundred years later, we are, however, still reluctant to accept this proposition. Even today such a statement would be regarded as highly cynical, despite the current fashion among reporters in the last part of the twentieth century to write what they believe the actions of a person to be, regardless of whether or not that person has actually behaved in that way. Meanwhile, there are whole areas of social behavior that go relatively unreported because we as a society are terrified to speak their names. We still look at people and assess their characters by what we *believe* to be the standards of our own characters. The dark sides of our characters are hidden, so we hide the dark sides of the characters whom we are trying to assess. We are fearful that by admitting the concealed side of another's character, we may be forced to accept that of our own. It is denying the dark side of human behavior that leads to trouble in any exchange with another person: politically, socially, legally, or commercially. All one shows when taking human fallibility into account is realism about the human condition. Machiavelli, in *The Prince,* showed no such fear of this shadowy side of human nature.

None of the three works in this volume promise solutions. Rather, they offer advice in their own way to assist those who have the determination to succeed on the track to self-fulfillment. When one compares Sun Tzu's *The Art of War* with *The Servant,* the former appears to be a book about warfare and the latter about service; but both are truly about human behavior. A man or a woman entering the world of politics, business, civil service, law, or even the arts should first learn about people. While none of these texts claims to be comprehensive in its understanding of people, this combined volume provides considerable insight into how people think and behave.

These works were all written for princes. *The Art of War* for He Lu, Prince of Wu, a man clearly content to let a strong general get on with the work of defending his state. Saved by this general, He Lu, for all his shortcomings in recognizing the importance of discipline, realized the necessity of employing a good general and after reading Sun Tzu's work, hired him immediately. Machiavelli wrote *The Prince* as a job application for Senior Advisor and Diplomat to Lorenzo de' Medici, a post he had already held in Florence. Whether Lorenzo ever read the book is a matter of conjecture, and Machiavelli did not get the job. The book is dedicated to Lorenzo, and although he was the final recipient of this brilliant work, it had been intended for Guiliano de' Medici, his uncle. Guiliano died and the manuscript was redirected.

The Servant was dedicated to a prince of a different kind—to the most magnificent Baroness Thatcher of Kesteven, Prime

Minister of Great Britain, 1979–1990, from one of her many servants who believes she could have been better served. A democratic leader or "prince," the Lady Thatcher needed to be served rather differently from Lorenzo de' Medici or Prince He Lu. In *The Servant,* I have followed in Machiavelli's tradition, trying my best to expose the reality of life rather than to obscure it with tidy phrases. *The Servant* came about as a result of my reading *The Prince* and concluding that the supreme servant, Machiavelli (not princely in any respect), was badly placed to advise princes. He would have been better placed advising the *servants* of princes, who in the 1980s were badly in need of advice. Those years in British politics were filled with treachery and turmoil. Despite the fact that Margaret Thatcher had often been the subject of insidious attacks, she had always survived. In 1980, members of the cabinet made a puerile attempt to overthrow their prime minister, then only one year in office. It was in that year that I began to write *The Servant.* After the incidents of 1980, the stage was set for a fight in the Machiavellian tradition: treachery following treachery for the next ten years. My anger in those days arose from the sheer injustice of that initial attack on Margaret Thatcher, and that was the first and last time I felt that emotion while in active politics. Anger has no place in politics or boxing; it only results in thoughtless attacks and a muddled defense. Concentrate all your energies not into anger but into determination. My book, *The Servant,* written in anger, was reworked and the anger tempered in 1991.* I used the style of Machiavelli's writing and his work *The Prince* as my model for the whole of *The Servant.* There is, however, one important difference between the approach to politics and so to life, both

---

*I had already served Margaret Thatcher for 15 years both as the Treasurer and Deputy Chairman.

commercial and private, in *The Prince* and *The Servant*. The latter is a work that tries to instruct servants on how best to help a prince carry out an idea. It was in fact a valedictory address, made to help and encourage successors. *The Servant* was not written with the hope of preferment; my prince was maliciously dismissed by her colleagues. I could not hope for benefit to flow from such people. I had retired from politics six months before Margaret Thatcher found herself with no honorable alternative but to resign the leadership of her party and so her post of prime minister. My retirement from politics fifteen years after I was first appointed to the Treasureship of the Conservative Party, came in time for me to witness the treachery that brought Margaret Thatcher down. No longer an official of her party, I should, I suppose, have taken an objective view of this event, if it is possible to take an objective view of treachery. For me, this betrayal was unforgivable, and the epilogue of *The Servant* chronicles the fall of Margaret Thatcher and the rise in general usage of her "idea," which, in a few words, was to roll back the control of the state and to set the people of Britain free providing them with a state that served them. Today, certain aspects of her policies, such as privatization of state industries, have spread across the world.

The Prince, The Servant, and *The Art of War* are in fact allegories—a joke, a revenge, and a plan of war. Each of them can be interpreted in a different way from that intended by its author. Each text is written in a style capable of many interpretations. Again, each work draws deeply on human nature as its inspiration and motive for being. *The Art of War* is inspirited by battles, positioning troops, and instilling discipline. *The Prince,* grounded in the actions of the ancients, counsels a person, whether a prince or a chairman, on how to rule. *The Servant* is inspired by the dramatic events of politics in Britain, at its best, under the rule of that country's greatest postwar leader. It is a work that glories in the notion of service, but only to a successful prince, showing how a servant can influence his employer and so in effect have power—in the form of influence, which when properly applied, is real power.

Each text is useful to the one working his or her way through any organization and to the person who could perhaps become its prince. Each is advantageous in its own right; together, they are formidable. All three are about the achievement of a stated aim or ambition. We, in the folly of our age, like to call the obtainment of that goal success when, in fact, it is whether you use a power and position merely for your own benefit or for the benefit of others that really matters—and sets the criteria by which you will one day be judged.

ALISTAIR MCALPINE

The Prince

NICOLO MACHIAVELLI

The Prince

NICOLO MACHIAVELLI TO THE MOST ILLUSTRIOUS
LORENZO, SON OF PIERO DE' MEDICI

Those who desire the favour of a prince do commonly introduce themselves by presenting him with such things as he either values much or does more than ordinarily delight in; for which reason he is frequently presented with horses, arms, cloth of gold, jewels, and such ornaments as are suitable to his quality and grandeur. Being ambitious to present myself to your Highness with some testimony of my devotions toward you, in all my wardrobe I could not find anything more precious (at least to myself) than the knowledge of the conduct and achievements of great men, which I learned by long conversation in modern affairs and a continual investigation of old. After long and diligent examination, having reduced all into a small volume, I do presume to present to your Highness; and though I cannot think it a work fit to appear in your presence, yet my confidence in your bounty is such, I hope it may be accepted, considering I was not capable of more than presenting you with a faculty of understanding in a short time, what for several years, with infinite labour and hazard, I had been gathering together. Nor have I beautified or adorned it with rhetorical ornations, or such outward embellishments as are usual in such descriptions. I had rather it should pass without any approbation than owe it to anything but the truth and gravity of the matter. I would not have it imputed to me as presumption, if an inferior person, as I am, pretend not only to treat of, but to prescribe and regulate the proceedings of princes; for, as they who take the landscape of a country, to consider the mountains and the nature of the higher places do descend ordinarily into the plains, and dispose themselves upon the hills to take the prospect of the valleys, in like manner, to understand the nature of the people it is necessary to be a prince, and to know the nature of princes it is as requisite to be of the people. May your Highness, then, accept this book with as much kindness as it is presented and if you please diligently and deliberately to reflect upon it you will find in it my extreme desire that your Highness may arrive at that grandeur which fortune and your accomplishments do seem to presage; from which pinnacle of honour, if your Highness vouchsafes at any time to look down upon things below, you will see how unjustly and how continually I have been exposed to the malignity of fortune.

CHAPTER I

The several sorts of Governments, and
after what manner they are obtained.

There never was nor is at this day any government in the world by which one man has rule and dominion over another, but it is either a commonwealth, or a monarchy. Monarchies are either hereditary, where the ancestors of the sovereign have been a long time in possession, or where they are but new. The new are either so wholly and entirely (as Milan was to Francis Sforza), or annexed to the hereditary dominions of the conqueror (as the kingdom of Naples to the kingdom of Spain). These territories thus acquired are accustomed either to be subject to some prince, or to live at liberty and free, and are subdued either by his auxiliaries or own forces, by his good fortune or conduct.

CHAPTER II

Of Hereditary Principalities.

I shall omit speaking of commonwealths, as having discoursed of them largely elsewhere, and write in this place only of principalities, and how, according to the foregoing division, the said principalities may be governed and maintained. I do affirm, then, that hereditary states, and such as have been accustomed to the family of their prince, are preserved with less difficulty than the new, and because it is sufficient not to transgress the examples of their predecessors, and next to comply and frame themselves to the accidents that occur. So that, if the prince be a person of competent industry, he will be sure to keep himself in the throne, unless he be supplanted by some great and more than ordinary force; and even then, when so supplanted, fortune can never turn tail, or be adverse to the usurper, but he will stand fair to be restored. Of this Italy affords us an example in the Duke of Ferrara, who supported bravely against the invasion of the Venetians in 1484, and afterwards against Pope Julius X., upon no other foundation but his antiquity in that government; for a natural prince has not so much occasion or necessity to oppress his subjects, whereby it follows he must be better beloved, and retain more of the affections of his people, unless some extraordinary vices concur to make him odious; so that the succession and coherence of his government takes away the causes and memory of innovations; for one new change leaves always (as in buildings) a toothing and aptitude of another.

CHAPTER III

Of Mixed Principalities.

But the difficulties consist in governments lately acquired, especially if not absolutely new, but as members annexed to the territories of the usurper, in which case such a government is called mixed. The tumults and revolutions in such monarchies proceed from a natural crossness and difficulty in all new conquests; for men do easily part with their prince upon hopes of bettering their condition, and that hope provokes them to rebel; but most commonly they are mistaken, and experience tells them their condition is much worse.

This proceeds from another natural and ordinary cause, necessitating the new prince to overlay or disgust his new subjects by quartering his army upon them, taxes, or a thousand other inconveniences, which are the perpetual consequents of conquest. So that you make them your enemies who suffer, and are injured by your usurpation, but cannot preserve their friendship who introduced you, because you are neither able to satisfy their expectation, or employ strong remedies against them, by reason of your obligations; wherefore, though an usurper be never so strong, and his army never so numerous, he must have intelligence with the natives if he means to conquer a province. For these reasons Louis XII. of France quickly subdued Milan, and lost it as quickly; for the same people which opened him their gates, finding themselves deceived in their hopes, and disappointed in the future benefits which they expected, could not brook nor comport with the haughtiness of their new sovereign: it is very true countries that have rebelled and are conquered the second time are recovered with more difficulty; for the defection of the people having taken off all obligation or respect from the usurper, he takes more liberty to secure himself by punishing offenders, exposing the suspected, and fortifying wherever he finds himself weak; so that Count Lodovick having been able to rescue Milan out of the hands of the French the first time only by harassing and infesting its borders, the second time he recovered it it was necessary for him to arm and confederate the whole world against the said king, and that his army should be beaten and driven out of Italy; and this happened from the aforesaid occasions: nevertheless the French were twice dispossessed. The general reasons of the first we have already discoursed, it remains now that we take a prospect of the second, and declare what remedies the said King Louis had, or what another may have in his condition, to preserve himself better in his new conquests than the King of France did before him. I say, then, that provinces newly acquired, and joined to the ancient territory of him who conquered them, are either of the same country, or language, or otherwise. In the first case they are easily kept, especially if the people have not been too much accustomed to liberty; and to secure the possession there needs no more than to extirpate the family of the prince which governed before; for in other things maintaining to them their old condition, there being no discrepancy in their customs, men do acquiesce and live quietly, as has been seen in the cases of Burgundy, Bretagne, Gascoigne, and Normandy, which have continued so long under the government of France; for though there be some difference in their language, nevertheless, their laws and customs being alike, they do easily consist. He therefore who acquires anything, and desires to preserve it, is obliged to have a care of two things more particularly; one is, that the family of the former prince be extinguished; the other, that no law or taxes be imposed: whereby it will come to pass, that in a short time it may be annexed and consolidated with his old principality. But where conquest is made in a country differing in language, customs and laws, there is the great difficulty; their good fortune and great industry is requisite to keep it. And one of the best and most efficacious expedients to do it would be for the usurper to live there himself, which would render his possession more secure and durable, as the great Turk has done in Greece, who, in despite of all his practices and policies to keep it in subjection, had he not fixed his imperial residence there would never have been able to have effected it. For being present in person, disorders are discovered in the bud and prevented, but being at a distance in some remote part, they come only by hearsay, and that, when they are got to a head, are commonly incurable. Besides, the province is not subject to be pillaged by officers, by reason of the nearness and accessibleness of their prince, which disposes those to love him who are good, and those to dread him who are otherwise; and if any foreigner attacks it, he must do it with more care and circumspection, in respect that the prince's residence being there it will be harder for him to lose it.

There is another remedy, rather better than worse, and that is, to plant colonies in one or two places, which may be as it were the keys of that State, and either that must be done of necessity, or an army of horse and foot be maintained in those parts, which is much worse; for colonies are of no great expense; the Prince sends and maintains them at very little charge, and intrenches only upon such as he is constrained to dispossess of their houses and land for the subsistence and accommodation of the new inhabitants, who are but few, and a small part of the State; they also who are injured and offended, living dispersed and in poverty, cannot do any mischief, and the rest being quiet and undisturbed, will not stir, lest they should mistake and run themselves into the same condition with their neighbours.

I conclude, likewise, that those colonies which are least chargeable are most faithful and inoffensive, and those few who are offended are too poor and dispersed to do any hurt, as I said before; and it is to be observed, men are either to be flattered and indulged or utterly destroyed*—because for small offences they do usually revenge themselves, but for great ones they cannot—so that injury is to be done in such a manner as not to fear any revenge. But if instead of colonies an army be kept on foot, it will be much more expensive, and the whole revenue of that province being consumed in the keeping it, the acquisition will be a loss, and rather a prejudice than otherwise, by removing the camp up and down the country, and changing their quarters, which is an inconvenience every man will resent and be ready to revenge, and they are the most dangerous and implacable enemies who are provoked by insolences committed against them in their own houses. In all respects, therefore, this kind of guard is unprofitable, whereas on the other side colonies are useful. Moreover, he who is in a province of a different constitution, as is said before, ought to make himself head and protector of his inferior neighbours, and endeavour with all diligence to weaken

---

* *Editor:* The most important sentence in the whole work and one from which Machiavelli's undesirable reputation springs.

and debilitate such as are more powerful, and to have a particular care that no stranger enters into the said province with as much power as he; for it will always happen that somebody or other will be invited by the malcontents, either out of ambition or fear. This is visible in the Etolians, who brought the Romans into Greece, who were never admitted into any province but by the temptation of the natives. The common method in such cases is this: as soon as a foreign potentate enters into a province, those who are weaker or disobliged join themselves with him out of emulation and animosity to those who are above them, insomuch that in respect of these inferior lords, no pains is to be omitted that may gain them; and when gained, they will readily and unanimously fall into one mass with the State that is conquered. Only the conqueror is to take special care they grow not too strong, nor be entrusted with too much authority, and then he can easily with his own forces and their assistance keep down the greatness of his neighbours, and make himself absolute arbiter in that province. And he who acts not this part prudently shall quickly lose what he has got, and even whilst he enjoys it be obnoxious to many troubles and inconveniences. The Romans in their new conquests observed this course, they planted their colonies, entertained the inferior lords into their protection without increasing their power; they kept under such as were more potent, and would not suffer any foreign prince to have interest among them. I will set down only Greece for an example. The Etolians and Achaians were protected, the kingdom of the Macedonians was depressed and Antiochus driven out; yet the merits and fidelity of the Achaians and Etolians could never procure them any increase of authority, nor the persuasions and applications of Philip induce the Romans to be his friends till he was overcome, nor the power of Antiochus prevail with them to consent that he should retain any sovereignty in that province: for the Romans acted in that case as all wise princes ought to do who are to have an eye not only upon present but future incommodities, and to redress them with all possible industry; for dangers that are seen afar off are easily prevented, but protracting till they are at hand, the remedies grow unseasonable and the malady incurable. And it falls out in this case, as the physicians say of an hectic fever, that at first it is easily cured and hard to be known, but in process of time, not being observed or resisted in the beginning, it becomes easy to be known but very difficult to be cured. So it is in matters of state, things which are discovered at a distance—which is done only by prudent men—produce little mischief but what is easily averted; but when through ignorance or inadvertency they come to that height that every one discerns them, there is no room for any remedy, and the disease is incurable. The Romans, therefore, foreseeing their troubles afar off, opposed themselves in time, and never swallowed any injury to put off a war, for they knew that war was not avoided but deferred thereby, and commonly with advantage to the enemy; wherefore they chose rather to make war upon Philip, and Antiochus in Greece, than suffer them to invade Italy; and yet at that time there was no necessity of either; they might have avoided them both, but they thought it not fit; for they could never relish the saying that is so frequent in the mouths of our new politicians "to enjoy the present benefit of time," but preferred the exercise of their courage and wisdom, for time carries all things along with it, and may bring good as well as evil, and ill as well as good. But let us return to France, and examine if what was there done was comfortable to what is prescribed here; and to this purpose I shall not speak of Charles VIII. but of Louis XII., as of a prince whose conduct and affairs (by reason his possession was longer in Italy) were more conspicuous, and you shall see how contrary he acted in everything that was necessary for the keeping of so different a State. This Louis was invited into Italy by the Venetians, who had an ambition to have got half Lombardy by his coming. I will not condemn the expedition, nor blame the counsels of that King for being desirous of footing in Italy, and having no allies left in that country, but all doors shut against him (upon the ill-treatment which his predecessor Charles had used towards them) he was constrained to take his friends where he could find them,★ and that resolution would have been lucky enough had he not miscarried in his other administration; for he had no sooner subdued Lombardy but he recovered all the reputation and dignity that was lost by King Charles. Genoa submitted, Florence courted his friendship, the Marquis of Mantua, the Duke of Ferrara, Bentivoglio, Madam de Furli, the Lords of Faenza, Pesoro, Rimini, Camerino, Piombino, the Lucchesi, Pisani, Sanesi, all of them address themselves to him for his alliance and amity; then the Venetians began to consider and reflect upon their indiscretion, who, to gain two towns in Lombardy, had made the King of France master of two-thirds of all Italy. Let any one now think with how little difficulty the said king might have kept up his reputation in that country if he had observed the rules aforesaid and protected his friends, who being numerous, and yet weak and fearful (some of the Pope, and some of the Venetians), were always under a necessity of standing by him, and with their assistance he might easily have secured himself against any competitor whatever. But he was no sooner in Milan but he began to prevaricate and send supplies to Pope Alexander to put him in possession of Romagna, not considering that thereby he weakened himself and disobliged his friends who had thrown themselves into his arms, and

---

★ *Editor:* The Florentine Machiavelli had a passionate hatred of the Venetians.

28

aggrandized the Church by adding to its spiritual authority★ (which was so formidable before) so great a proportion of temporal; and having committed one error, he was forced to proceed so far as to put a stop to the ambition of Pope Alexander, and hinder his making himself master of Tuscany; the said Louis was forced into Italy again. Nor was it enough for him to have advanced the interest of the Church and deserted his friends, but out of an ardent desire to the kingdom of Naples he shared it with the King of Spain; so that whereas before he was sole umpire in Italy, he now entertained a partner, to whom the ambitious of that province and his own malcontents might repair upon occasion; and whereas the King of that kingdom might have been made his pensioner, he turned out him to put in another that might be able to turn out himself.†

It is very obvious, and no more than natural, for princes to desire to extend their dominion, and when they attempt nothing but what they are able to achieve they are applauded, at least not upbraided thereby; but when they are unable to compass it, and yet will be doing, then they are condemned, and indeed not unworthily.

If France, then, with its own forces alone, had been able to have enterprised upon Naples, it ought to have been done; but if her own private strength was too weak, it ought not to have been divided: and if the division of Lombardy, to which he consented with the Venetian, was excusable, it was because done to get footing in Italy; but this partition of Naples with the King of Spain is extremely to be condemned, because not

---

★ *Editor:* Machiavelli was also censorious of the Church's temporal power—in his last words he expressed the desire to go to Hell, for that is where he believed that he would find popes, cardinals, and princes.

† *Editor:* Machiavelli would have preferred the French King to be the ally of Florence rather than all the others.

pressed or quickened by such necessity as the former. Louis therefore committed five faults in this expedition. He ruined the inferior lords; he augmented the dominion of a neighbour prince; he called in a foreigner as puissant as himself; he neglected to continue there in person; and planted no colonies— all which errors might have been no inconvenience whilst he had lived, had he not been guilty of a sixth, and that was depressing the power of the Venetian. If indeed he had not sided with the Church, nor brought the Spaniards into Italy, it had been but reasonable for him to have taken down the pride of the Venetian; but pursuing his first resolutions, he ought not to have suffered them to be ruined, because whilst the Venetian strength was entire, they would have kept off other people from attempting upon Lombardy, to which the Venetian would never have consented, unless upon condition it might have been delivered to them, and the others would not in probability have forced it from France to have given it to them; and to have contended with them both nobody would have had the courage. If it be urged that King Louis gave up Romagna to the Pope, and the kingdom of Naples to the King of Spain, to evade a war, I answer, as before, that a present mischief is not to be suffered to prevent a war, for the war is not averted but protracted, and will follow with greater disadvantage.

If the King's faith and engagements to the Pope to undertake this enterprise for him be objected, and that he did it to recompense the dissolution of his marriage, and the cap which at his intercession his Holiness had conferred upon the Legate of Amboise, I refer them for an answer to what I shall say hereafter about the faith of a prince, how far it obliges. So then King Louis lost Lombardy because he did not observe one of those rules which others have followed with success in the conquest of provinces, and in their desire to keep them; nor is it an extraordinary thing, but what happens every day, and not without reason. To this purpose, I remember I was once in discourse with the Cardinal d'Amboise at Nantes, at the time when Valentino (for so Cæsar Borgia, Pope Alexander's son was commonly called) possessed himself of Romagna. In the heat of our conference, the Cardinal telling me that the Italians were ignorant of the art of war, I replied that the French had as little skill in matters of State; for if they had had the least policy in the world they would never have suffered the Church to have come to that height and elevation. And it has been found since by experience, that the grandeur of the Church and the Spaniard in Italy is derived from France, and that they in requital have been the ruin and expulsion of the French.

From hence a general rule may be deduced, and such a one as seldom or never is subject to exception,—viz., that whoever is the occasion of another's advancement is the cause of his own diminution; because that advancement is founded either upon the conduct or power of the donor, either of which becomes suspicious at length to the person preferred.*

CHAPTER IV

*Why the Kingdom of Darius,
usurped by Alexander, did not rebel against
his Successors, after Alexander was dead.*

The difficulties encountered in the keeping of a new conquest being considered, it may well be admired how it came to pass

---

* *Editor:* A fine example of Machiavelli's ironical approach to life. Four hundred years later, the British poet, Oscar Wilde, expressed the same sentiments when he wrote, "A good turn never goes unpunished."

that Alexander the Great, having in a few years made himself master of Asia, and died as soon as he had done, that State could be kept from rebellion; yet his successors enjoyed it a long time peaceably without any troubles or concussions but what sprung from their own avarice and ambition. I answer that all monarchies of which we have any record were governed after two several manners; either by a prince and his servants who he vouchsafes out of his mere grace to constitute his ministers, and admits of their assistance in the government of his kingdom; or else by a prince and his barons, who were persons advanced to that quality, not by favour or concession of the prince, but by the ancientness and nobility of their extraction. These barons have their proper jurisdictions and subjects, who own their authority and pay them a natural respect. Those States which are governed by the prince and his servants have their prince more arbitrary and absolute, because his supremacy is acknowledged by everybody; and if another be obeyed, it is only as his minister and substitute, without any affection to the man. Examples of these different governments we may find in our time in the persons of the Grand Signor and the King of France. The whole Turkish monarchy is governed by a single person, the rest are but his servants and slaves; for distinguishing his whole monarchy into provinces and governments (which they call Sangiacchi) he sends when and what officers he thinks fit, and changes them as he pleases. But the King of France is established in the middle, as it were, of several great lords, whose sovereignty having been owned, and families beloved a long time by their subjects, they keep their pre-eminence; nor is it in the king's power to deprive them without inevitable danger to himself. He, therefore, who considers the one with the other will find the Turkish empire harder to be subdued; but when once conquered more easy to be kept. The reason of the difficulty is, because the usurper cannot be called in by the grandees of the empire, nor hope any assistance from the great officers to facilitate his enterprise, which proceeds from the reasons aforesaid; for being all slaves and under obligation they are not easily corrupted; and if they could, little good was to be expected from them, being unable for the aforesaid reasons to bring them any party: so that whoever invades the Turk must expect to find him entire and united, and is to depend more upon his own proper force than any disorders among them; but having once conquered them, and beaten their army beyond the possibility of a recruit, the danger is at an end; for there is nobody remaining to be afraid of but the family of the emperor, which, being once extinguished, nobody else has any interest with the people, and they are as little to be apprehended after the victory as they were to be relied upon before. But in kingdoms that are governed according to the model of France it happens quite contrary, because having gained some of the barons to your side (and some of them will always be discontented and desirous of change), you may readily enter; they can, as I said before, give you easy admission and contribute to your victory. But to defend and make good what you have got brings a long train of troubles and calamities with it, as well upon your friends as your foes. Nor will it suffice to exterminate the race of the king; forasmuch as other princes will remain, who, upon occasion, will make themselves heads of any commotion, and they being neither to be satisfied nor extinguished, you must of necessity be expelled upon the first insurrection.

Now, if it be considered what was the nature of Darius's government, it will be found to have been very like the Turks, and therefore Alexander was obliged to fight them, and having conquered them, and Darius dying after the victory, the empire of the Persians remained quietly to Alexander, for the reasons aforesaid; and his successors, had they continued united, might have enjoyed it in peace, for in that whole empire no tumults succeeded but what were raised by themselves. But in kingdoms that are constituted like France it is otherwise, and impossible to possess them in quiet. From hence sprung the many defections of Spain, France and Greece from the Romans, by reason of the many little principalities in those several kingdoms of which, whilst there remained any memory, the Romans enjoyed their possession in a great deal of uncertainty; but when their memory was extinct by power and diuturnity of empire, they grew secure in their possessions, and quarrelling afterwards among themselves, every officer of the Romans was able to bring a party into the field, according to the latitude and extent of his command in the said provinces; and the reason was, because the race of their old princes being extirpate, there was nobody left for them to acknowledge but the Romans. These things, therefore, being considered, it is not to be wondered that Alexander had the good fortune to keep the empire of Asia, whilst the rest, as Pyrrhus and others, found such difficulty to retain what they had got; for it came not to pass from the small or great virtue of the victor, but from the difference and variety of the subject.

CHAPTER V

How such Cities and Principalities are to be governed who lived under their own Laws before they were subdued.

When States that are newly conquered have been accustomed to their liberty, and lived under their own laws, to keep them three ways are to be observed: the first is utterly to ruin them; the second, to live personally among them; the third is (contenting

34

yourself with a pension from them) to permit them to enjoy their old privileges and laws, erecting a kind of Council of State, to consist of a few which may have a care of your interest, and keep the people in amity and obedience. And that Council being set up by you, and knowing that it subsists only by your favour and authority, will not omit anything that may propagate and enlarge them. A town that has been anciently free cannot more easily be kept in subjection than by employing its own citizens, as may be seen by the example of the Spartans and Romans. The Spartans had got possession of Athens and Thebes, and settled an oligarchy according to their fancy; and yet they lost them again. The Romans, to keep Capua, Carthage and Numantia, ordered them to be destroyed, and they kept them by that means. Thinking afterwards to preserve Greece, as the Spartans had done, by allowing them their liberty, and indulging their old laws, they found themselves mistaken; so that they were forced to subvert many cities in that province before they could keep it; and certainly that is the safest way which I know; for whoever conquers a free town and does not demolish it commits a great error, and may expect to be ruined himself;* because whenever the citizens are disposed to revolt, they betake themselves of course to that blessed name of liberty, and the laws of their ancestors, which no length of time nor kind usage whatever will be able to eradicate; and let all possible care and provision be made to the contrary, unless they be divided some way or other, or the inhabitants dispersed, the thought of their old privileges will never out of their heads, but upon all occasions they will endeavour to recover them, as Pisa did after it had continued so many years in subjection to the Florentines. But it falls out quite contrary where the cities or

---

* *Editor:* A fine example of Machiavelli's advocacy of a ruthless approach to the business of governing colonies.

provinces have been used to a prince whose race is extirpated and gone; for being on the one side accustomed to obey, and on the other at a loss for their old family, they can never agree to set up another, and will never know how to live freely without; so that they are not easily to be tempted to rebel, and the prince may oblige them with less difficulty, and be secure of them when he hath done. But in a commonwealth their hatred is more inveterate, their revenge more insatiable; nor does the memory of their ancient liberty ever suffer, or ever can suffer them to be quiet; so that the most secure way is either to ruin them quite, or make your residence among them.*

CHAPTER VI

*Of Principalities acquired by one's
own proper conduct and arms.*

Let no man think it strange if in speaking of new governments, either by princes or states, I introduce great and eminent examples; forasmuch as men in their actions follow commonly the ways that are beaten, and when they would do any generous thing they propose to themselves some pattern of that nature; nevertheless, being impossible to come up exactly to that, or to acquire that virtue in perfection which you desire to imitate; a wise man ought always to set before him for his example the actions of great men who have excelled in the achievement of some great exploit, to the end that though his virtue and power arrives not at that perfection, it may at least come as near as is

---

* *Editor:* In this passage, Machiavelli accurately describes the Nationalist movements of the 20th century.

possible, and receive some tincture thereby. Like experienced archers, who observing the mark to be at great distance, and knowing the strength of their bow, and how far it will carry, they fix their aim somewhat higher than the mark, not with design to shoot at that height, but that by mounting their arrow to a certain proportion, they may come the nearer to the mark they intend. I say, then, that principalities newly acquired by an upstart prince are more or less difficult to maintain, as he is more or less provident that gains them. And because the happiness of rising from a private person to be a prince presupposes great virtue or fortune, where both of them concur they do much facilitate the conservation of the conquest; yet he who has committed least to fortune has continued the longest. It prevents much trouble likewise, when the prince (having no better residence elsewhere) is constrained to live personally among them. But to speak of such who by their virtue, rather than fortune, have advanced themselves to that dignity, I say that the most renowned and excellent are Moses, Cyrus, Romulus, Theseus, and the like. And though Moses might be reasonably excepted, as being only the executioner of God's immediate commands, yet he deserves to be mentioned, if it were only for that grace which rendered him capable of communication with God. But if we consider Cyrus, and the rest of the conquerors and founders of monarchies, we shall find them extraordinary; and examining their lives and exploits, they will appear not much different from Moses, who had so incomparable a Master; for by their conversations and successes they do not seem to have received anything from fortune but occasion and opportunity, in introducing what forms of government they pleased; and as without that occasion the greatness of their courage had never been known, so had not they been magnanimous, and taken hold of it, that occasion had happened in vain. It was necessary, therefore, for Moses that the people of Israel should be in captivity in Egypt that to free themselves from bondage they might be disposed to follow him. It was convenient that Romulus should be turned out of Albo, and exposed to the wild beasts when he was young, that he might afterwards be made King of Rome, and founder of that great empire. It was not unnecessary, likewise, that Cyrus should find the Persians mutinying at the tyranny of the Medes, and that the Medes should be grown soft and effeminate with their long peace. Theseus could never have given proof of his virtue and generosity had not the Athenians been in great trouble and confusion. These great advantages made those great persons eminent, and their great wisdom knew how to improve them to the reputation and enlargement of their country. They, then, who become great by the ways of virtue (as the princes aforesaid) do meet with many difficulties before they arrive at their ends, but having compassed them once they easily keep them. The difficulties in the acquisition arise in part from new laws and customs which they are forced to introduce for the establishment and security of their own dominion; and this is to be considered, that there is nothing more difficult to undertake, more uncertain to succeed, and more dangerous to manage, than to make one's self prince, and prescribe new laws. Because he who innovates in that manner has for his enemies all those who made any advantage by the old laws; and those who expect benefit by the new will be but cool and lukewarm in his defence; which lukewarmness proceeds from a certain awe for their adversaries, who have their old laws on their side, and partly from a natural incredulity in mankind, which gives credit but slowly to any new thing,★

★ *Editor:* Today the situation is drastically different with a great reverence paid to the new than ever before. This, however, is a phenomenon of the late quarter of the 20th century.

unless recommended first by the experiment of success. Hence it proceeds, that the first time the adversary has opportunity to make an attempt, he does it with great briskness and vigour; but the defence is so trepid and faint, that for the most part the new prince and his adherents perish together. Wherefore for better discussion of this case it is necessary to inquire whether these innovators do stand upon their own feet, or depend upon other people; that is to say, whether in the conduct of their affairs they do make more use of their rhetoric than their arms. In the first case they commonly miscarry, and their designs seldom succeed; but when their expectations are only from themselves, and they have power in their own hands to make themselves obeyed, they run little or no hazard, and do frequently prevail. For further eviction, the Scripture shows us that those of the prophets whose arms were in their hands, and had power to compel, succeeded better in the reformations which they designed; whereas those who came only with exhortation and good language suffered martyrdom and banishment, because (besides the reasons aforesaid) the people are inconstant and susceptible of any new doctrine at first, but not easily brought to retain it; so that things are to be ordered in such manner that when their faith begins to stagger they may be forced to persist. Moses, Cyrus, Theseus, and Romulus could never have made their laws to have been long observed had they not had power to have compelled it;★ as in our days it happened to Friar Jerome Savonarola, who ruined himself by his new institutions as soon as the people of Florence began to desert him, for he had no means to confirm them who had been of his opinion, nor to constrain such as dissented. Wherefore such persons meet with great difficulty in

---

★ *Editor:* Military force, Machiavelli argues, is an encouragement to make people pay attention to your views.

their affairs; all their dangers are still by the way, which they can hardly overcome, but by some extraordinary virtue and excellence; nevertheless, when once they have surmounted them, and arrived at any degree of veneration, having supplanted those who envied their advancement, they remain puissant and firm, and honourable and happy. I will add to these great examples another, perhaps not so conspicuous, but one that will bear a proportion and resemblance with the rest, and shall satisfy me for all others of that nature. It is of Hiero of Syracuse, who of a private person was made prince of that city, for which he was beholding to fortune no further than for the occasion, because the Syracusans being under oppression chose him for their captain, in which command he behaved himself so well he deserved to be made their prince, for he was a person of so great virtue and excellence that those who have written of him have given him this character, that even in his private condition he wanted nothing but a kingdom to make him an admirable king. This Hiero subdued the old militia, established a new; renounced the old allies, confederated with others, and having friends and forces of his own, he was able upon such a foundation to erect what fabric he pleased, so that though the acquisition cost him much trouble he maintained it with little.

CHAPTER VII

Of new Principalities acquired by accident
and the supplies of other people.

They who from private condition ascend to be princes, and merely by the indulgence of fortune, arrive without much trouble at their dignity, though it costs them dear to maintain it, meet but little difficulty in their passage, being hurried as it were with wings, yet when they come to settle and establish then begins their misery. These kind of persons are such as attain their dignity by bribes, or concession of some other great prince, as it happened to several in Greece, in the cities of Ionia, and upon the Hellespont, where they were invested with that power by Darius for his greater security and glory, and to those emperors who arrived at the empire by the corruption of the soldiers. These persons, I say, subsist wholly upon the pleasure and fortune of those who advanced them, which being two things very valuable and uncertain, they have neither knowledge nor power to continue long in that degree; know not, because, unless he be a man of extraordinary qualities and virtue, it is not reasonable to think he can know how to command other people, who before lived always in a private condition himself; cannot, because they have no forces upon whose friendship and fidelity they can rely. Moreover, States which are suddenly conquered (as all things else in Nature whose rise and increase is so speedy) can have no root or foundation but what will be shaken and supplanted by the first gust of adversity, unless they who have been so suddenly exalted be so wise as to prepare prudently in time for the conservation of what fortune threw so luckily into their lap, and establish afterwards such fundamentals for their duration as others (which I mentioned before) have done in the like cases. About the arrival at this authority either by virtue, or good fortune, I shall instance in two examples that are fresh in our memory; one is Francis Sforza, the other Cæsar Borgia; Sforza, by just means and extraordinary virtue, made himself Duke of Milan, and enjoyed it in great peace, though gained with much trouble. Borgia, on the other side (called commonly Duke of Valentine), got several fair territories by the fortune of his father Pope Alexander, and lost them all after his death, though he used all his industry, and employed all the arts which a wise and brave prince ought to do to fix himself in the sphere where the arms and fortune of other people had placed him: for he, as I said before, who laid not his foundation in time, may yet raise his superstructure, but with great trouble to the architect and great danger to the building. If, therefore, the whole progress of the said Duke be considered, it will be found what solid foundations he had laid for his future dominion, of which progress I think it not superfluous to discourse, because I know not what better precepts to display before a new prince than the example of his actions; and though his own orders and methods did him no good, it was not so much his fault as the malignity of his fortune.★

Pope Alexander the Sixth had a desire to make his son Duke Valentine great, but he saw many blocks and impediments in the way, both for the present and future. First, he could not see any way to advance him to any territory that depended not upon the Church; and to those in his gift he was sure the Duke of Milan and the Venetians would never consent; for Faenza and Riminum had already put themselves under the Venetian protection. He was likewise sensible that the forces of Italy, especially those who were capable of assisting him, were in the hands of those who ought to apprehend the greatness of the Pope, as the Ursini, Colonnesi, and their followers, and therefore could not repose any great confidence in them; besides, the laws and alliances of all the States in Italy must of necessity be disturbed before he could make himself master of any part, which was no hard matter to do, finding the Venetians, upon

---

★ *Editor:* Machiavelli accepts that luck affects success and in Chapter 25 describes to what extent this happens. Oscar Wilde, the 19th century British poet said, "Success is entirely due to luck. Ask any failure."

some private interest of their own, inviting the French to another expedition into Italy, which his Holiness was so far from opposing that he promoted it by dissolution of King Louis's former marriage.* Louis therefore passed the Alps by the assistance of the Venetians and Alexander's consent, and was no sooner in Milan but he sent forces to assist the Pope in his enterprise against Romagna, which was immediately surrendered upon the king's reputation. Romagna being in this manner reduced by the Duke, and the Colonnesi defeated, being ambitious not only to keep what he had got, but to advance in his conquests, two things obstructed: one was the infidelity of his own army, the other the aversion of the French; for he was jealous of the forces of the Ursini who were in his service, suspected they would fail him in his need, and either hinder his conquest or take it from him when he had done; and the same fears he had of the French. And his jealousy of the Ursini was much increased when, after the expugnation of Faenza, assaulting Bologna, he found them very cold and backward in the attack. And the King's inclination he discovered when, having possessed himself of the Duchy of Urbin, he invaded Tuscany, and was by him required to desist. Whereupon the Duke resolved to depend no longer upon fortune and foreign assistance, and the first course he took was to weaken the party of the Ursini and Colonni in Rome, which he effected very neatly by debauching such of their adherents as were gentlemen, taking them into his own service, and giving them honourable pensions and governments and commands, according to their respective qualities; so that in a few months their passion for that faction evaporated, and they turned all for the Duke. After this he attended an opportunity of supplanting the Ursini, as he had done the family of the Colonni before,

---

* *Editor:* Machiavelli takes another dig at the Venetians and the French.

which happened very luckily, and was as luckily improved: for the Ursini, considering too late that the greatness of the Duke and the Church tended to their ruin, held a council at a place called Magione, in Perugia, which occasioned the rebellion of Urbin, the tumults in Romagna, and a thousand dangers to the Duke besides; but though he overcame them all by the assistance of the French, and recovered his reputation, yet he grew weary of his foreign allies, as having nothing further to oblige them, and betook himself to his artifice, which he managed so dexterously that the Ursini reconciled themselves to him by the mediation of Seignor Paulo, with whom for his security he comported so handsomely by presenting with money, rich stuffs,★ and horses, that being convinced of his integrity, he conducted them to Sinigaglia, and delivered them into the Duke's hands. Having by this means exterminated the chief of his adversaries, and reduced their friends, the Duke had laid a fair foundation for his greatness, having gained Romagna and the Duchy of Urbin, and insinuated with the people by giving them a gust of their future felicity. And because this part is not unworthy to be known for imitation sake, I will not pass it in silence. When the Duke had possessed himself of Romagna, finding it had been governed by poor and inferior lords, who had rather robbed than corrected their subjects, and given them more occasion of discord than unity, insomuch as that province was full of robberies, riots, and all manner of insolencies; to reduce them to unanimity and subjection to monarchy, he thought it necessary to provide them a good governor, and thereupon he conferred that charge upon Remiro d'Orco, with absolute power, though he was a cruel and passionate man. Orco was not long before he had settled it in peace, with no small

---

★ *Editor:* Silks and other materials.

reputation to himself. Afterwards, the Duke, apprehending so large a power might grow odious to the people, he erected a court of judicature in the middle of the province, in which every city had its advocate, and an excellent person was appointed to preside. And because he discovered that his past severity had created him many enemies, to remove that ill opinion, and recover the affections of the people, he had a mind to show that, if any cruelty had been exercised, it proceeded not from him but from the arrogance of his minister; and for their further confirmation, he caused the said governor to be apprehended, and his head chopped off one morning in the marketplace at Cesena, with a wooden dagger on one side of him and a bloody knife on the other; the ferocity of which spectacle not only appeased but amazed the people for a while. But resuming our discourse, I say, the Duke finding himself powerful enough, and secure against present danger, being himself as strong as he desired, and his neighbours in a manner reduced to an incapacity of hurting him, being willing to go on with his conquests, there remaining nothing but a jealousy of France, and not without cause, for he knew that king had found his error at last, and would be sure to obstruct him. Hereupon he began to look abroad for new allies, and to hesitate and stagger towards France, as appeared when the French army advanced into the kingdom of Naples against the Spaniards, who had besieged Cajeta. His great design was to secure himself against the French, and he had doubtless done it if Alexander had lived. These were his provisions against the dangers that were imminent; but those that were remote were more doubtful and uncertain. The first thing he feared was lest the next Pope should be his enemy, and reassume all that Alexander had given him, to prevent which he proposed four several ways. The first was by destroying the whole line of those lords whom he had dispossessed, that his

Holiness might have no occasion to restore them. The second was to cajole the nobility in Rome, and draw them over to his party, that thereby he might put an awe and restraint upon the Pope. The third was, if possible, to make the College his friends. The fourth was to make himself so strong before the death of his father as to be able to stand upon his own legs and repel the first violence that should be practised against him. Three of these four expedients he had tried before Alexander died, and was in a fair way for the fourth; all the disseized lords which came into his clutches he put to death, and left few of them remaining; he had insinuated with the nobility of Rome, and got a great party in the College of Cardinals; and as to his own corroboration, he had designed to make himself master of Tuscany, had got possession of Perugia and Piombino already, and taken Pisa into his protection. And having now farther regard of the French (who were beaten out of the kingdom of Naples by the Spaniard, and both of them reduced to necessity of seeking his amity), he leaped bluntly into Pisa, after which Lucca and Sienna submitted without much trouble, partly in hatred to the Florentines, and partly for fear; and the Florentines were grown desperate and without any hopes of relief; so that had these things happened before, as they did the same year in which Alexander died, doubtless he had gained so much strength and reputation that he would have stood firm by himself upon the basis of his own power and conduct, without depending upon fortune or any foreign supplies. But his father died five years after his son had taken up arms, and left him nothing solid and in certainty, but Romagna only, and the rest were *in nubibus,* infested with two formidable armies, and himself mortally sick. This Duke was a man of that magnanimity and prudence, understood so well which way men were to

be wheedled,★ or destroyed, and such were the foundations that
he had laid in a short time, that had he not had those two great
armies upon his back, and a fierce distemper upon his body, he
had overcome all difficulties and brought his designs to perfection. That the foundations which he had laid were plausible appeared by the patience of his subjects in Romagna, who held
out for him a complete month, though they knew he was at
death's door, and unlikely ever to come out of Rome, to which
place, though the Baglioni, the Vitelli, and the Ursini returned,
seeing there was no likelihood of his recovery, yet they could
not gain any of his party, nor debauch them to their side. It is
possible he was not able to put who he pleased into the Pontifical chair, yet he had power enough to keep any man out who
he thought was his enemy; but had it been his fortune to have
been well when his father Alexander died, all things had succeeded to his mind. He told me himself, about the time that
Julius XI. was created, that he had considered well the accidents
that might befall him upon the death of his father, and provided against them all, only he did not imagine that at his death
he should be so near it himself. Upon serious examination,
therefore, of the whole conduct of Duke Valentine, I see nothing to be reprehended; it seems rather proper to me to propose
him, as I have done, as an example for the imitation of all such
as by the favour of fortune, or the supplies of other princes,
have got into the saddle; for his mind being so large, and his intentions so high, he could not do otherwise, and nothing could
have opposed the greatness and wisdom of his designs but his
own infirmity and the death of his father. He, therefore, who
thinks it necessary in the minority of his dominion to secure

---

★ *Editor:* To wheedle is to manipulate.

himself against his enemies, to gain himself friends; to overcome, whether by force or by fraud; to make himself beloved or feared by his people; to be followed and reverenced by his soldiers; to destroy and exterminate such as would do him injury; to repeal and suppress old laws, and introduce new; to be severe, grateful, magnanimous, liberal, cashier and disband such of his army as were unfaithful, and put new in their places; manage himself so in his alliances with kings and princes that all of them should be either obliged to requite him or afraid to offend him: he, I say, cannot find a fresher or better model than the actions of this prince. If in anything he is to be condemned, it is in suffering the election of Julius IX., which was much to his prejudice; for though, as is said before, he might be unable to make the Pope as he pleased, yet it was in his power to have put any one by, and he ought never to have consented to the election of any of the cardinals whom he had formerly offended, or who, after their promotion, were like to be jealous of him; for men are as mischievous for fear as for hatred. Those cardinals which he had disobliged were, among others, the cardinals of St. Peter ad Vincula, Collonno St. George, and Ascanius. The rest, if any of them were advanced to the Papacy, might well be afraid of him, except the Spanish cardinals and the cardinal of Roan; the Spaniards by reason of their obligations and alliance, and the other by reason of his interest in the kingdom of France. Wherefore, above all things, the Duke should have made a Spanish cardinal Pope; and if that could not have been done, he should rather have consented to the election of Roan than St. Peter ad Vincula; for it is weakness to believe that among great persons new obligations can obliterate old injuries and disgusts. So that in the election of this Julius XI. Duke Valentine committed an error that was the cause of his utter destruction.

CHAPTER VIII

Of such as have arrived at their Dominion
by wicked and unjustifiable means.

Now because there are two ways from a private person to become a prince, which ways are not altogether to be attributed
either to fortune or management, I think it not convenient to
pretermit them, though of one of them I may speak more largely
where occasion is offered to treat more particularly of Republics.
One of the ways is, when one is advanced to the sovereignty by
any illegal nefarious means; the other, when a citizen by the
favour and partiality of his fellow-citizens is made prince of his
country. I shall speak of the first in this chapter, and justify what
I say by two examples, one ancient, the other modern, without
entering further into the merits of the cause, as judging them
sufficient for any man who is necessitated to follow them.
Agathocles, the Sicilian, not only from a private, but from a vile
and abject, condition was made king of Syracuse; and being but
the son of a potter, he continued the dissoluteness of his life
through all the degrees of his fortune; nevertheless, his vices
were accompanied with such courage and activity that he applied
himself to the wars, by which, and his great industry, he came at
length to the pretor of Syracuse. Being settled in that dignity,
and having concluded to make himself prince, and hold that by
violence, without obligation to anybody, which was conferred
upon him by consent, he settled an intelligence with Amilcar the
Carthaginian, who was then at the head of an army in Sicily, and
calling the people and Senate of Syracuse together one morning,
as if he had been to consult them in some matter of importance
to the State, upon a signal appointed he caused all his soldiers to

kill all the senators and the most wealthy of the people; after whose death he usurped and possessed the dominion of that city without any obstruction; and though afterwards he lost two great battles to the Carthaginians, and at length was besieged, yet he was not only able to defend that city, but leaving part of his forces for the security of that, with the rest he transported into Africa, and ordered things so that in a short time he relieved Syracuse, and reduced the Carthaginians into such extreme necessity that they were glad to make peace with him, and contenting themselves with Africa, leave Sicily to Agathocles. He then who examines the exploits and conduct of Agathocles will find little or nothing that may be attributed to fortune, seeing he rose not, as is said before, by the favour of any man, but by the steps and gradations of war, with a thousand difficulties and dangers having gotten that government, which he maintained afterwards with as many noble achievements. Nevertheless it cannot be called virtue in him to kill his fellow-citizens, betray his friends, to be without faith, without pity, or religion; these are ways may get a man empire, but no glory or reputation. Yet if the wisdom of Agathocles be considered, his dexterity in encountering and overcoming of dangers, his courage in supporting and surmounting his misfortunes, I do not see why he should be held inferior to the best captains of his time. But his unbounded cruelty and barbarous inhumanity, added to a million of other vices, will not permit that he be numbered amongst the most excellent men. So then, that which he performed cannot justly be attributed to either fortune or virtue; for he did all himself, without either the one or the other. In our days, under the Papacy of Alexander VI., Oliverotto da Fermo being left young many years since by his parents, was brought up by his uncle by the mother's side, called John Fogliani, and in his youth listed a soldier under Paulo Vitelli, that having improved himself by his discipline, he might be capable of some eminent command. Paulo being dead, he served under Vitellezzo, his brother, and in a short time by the acuteness of his parts and the briskness of his courage, became one of the best officers in his army. But thinking it beneath him to continue in any man's service, he conspired with some of his fellow-citizens of Fermo (to whom the servitude of their country was more agreeable than its liberty) by the help of Vitellesco to seize upon Fermo. In order to which, he wrote a letter to his uncle John Fogliano, importing that, having been absent many years, he had thoughts of visiting him and Fermo, and taking some little diversion in the place where he was born, and because the design of his service had been only the gaining of honour, that his fellow-citizens might see his time had not been ill-spent, he desired admission for a hundred horse of his friends and his equipage, and begged of him that he would take care they might be honourably received, which would redound not only to his honour, but his uncle's, who had had the bringing him up. John was not wanting in any office to his nephew; and having caused him to be nobly received, he lodged him in his own house, where he continued some days, preparing in the meantime what was necessary to the execution of his wicked design. He made a great entertainment, to which he invited John Fogliani and all the chief citizens in the town. About the end of the treatment when they were entertaining one another, as is usual at such times, Oliverotto very subtilely promoted certain grave discourses about the greatness of Pope Alexander and Cæsar his son, and of their designs. John and the rest replying freely to what was said, Oliverotto smiled, and told them those were points to be argued more privately, and thereupon removing into a chamber, his uncle and the rest of his fellow-citizens followed. They were scarce sat down before soldiers (which were concealed about the room) came forth and killed all of them, and the uncle among the rest. After the murder was committed, Oliverotto mounted on horseback, rode about, and rummaged the whole town, having besieged the chief magistrate in his palace; so that for fear all people submitted, and he established a government of which he made himself head. Having put such to death as were discontented, and in any capacity of doing him hurt, he fortified himself with new laws, both military and civil, insomuch as in a year's time he had not only fixed himself in Fermo, but was become terrible to all that were about him; and he would have been as hard as Agathocles to be supplanted, had he not suffered himself to have been circumvented by Cæsar Borgia, when at Singalia (as aforesaid) he took the Ursini and Vitelli; where also he himself was taken a year after his parricide was committed, and strangled with his master Vitellozzo, from whom he had learned all his good qualities and evil.

It may seem wonderful to some people how it should come to pass that Agathocles, and such as he, after so many treacheries and acts of inhumanity, should live quietly in their own country so long, defend themselves so well against foreign enemies, and none of their subjects conspire against them at home, seeing several others, by reason of their cruelty, have not been able, even in times of peace as well as war, to defend their government. I conceive it fell out according as their cruelty was well or ill applied; I say well applied (if that word may be added to an ill action), and it may be called so when committed but once, and that of necessity for one's own preservation, but never repeated afterwards, and even then converted as much as possible to the benefit of the subjects. Ill applied are such cruelties as are but few in the beginning, but in time do rather multiply than decrease. Those who are guilty of the first do receive assistance sometimes both from God and man, and Agathocles is an instance. But the others cannot possibly subsist long. From whence it is to be observed, that he who usurps the government of any State is to execute and put in practice all the cruelties which he thinks material at once, that he may have no occasion to renew them often, but that by his discontinuance he may mollify the people, and by his benefits bring them over to his side. He who does otherwise, whether for fear or ill counsel, is obliged to be always ready with his knife in his hand; for he can never repose any confidence in his subjects, whilst they, by reason of his fresh and continued inhumanities, cannot be secure against him. So then injuries are to be committed all at once, that the last being the less, the distaste may be likewise the less; but benefits should be distilled by drops, that the relish may be the greater. Above all, a prince is so to behave himself towards his subjects that neither good fortune nor bad should be able to alter him; for being once assaulted with adversity, you have no time to do mischief; and the good which you do, does you no good, being looked upon as forced, and so no thanks to be due for it.

CHAPTER IX

Of Civil Principality.

I shall speak now of the other way, when a principal citizen, not by wicked contrivance or intolerable violence, is made sovereign of his country, which may be called a civil principality, and is not to be attained by either virtue or fortune alone, but by a lucky sort of craft; this man, I say, arrives at the government by the favour of the people or nobility, for in all cities the meaner and the better sort of citizens are of different humours, and it proceeds from hence that the common people are not willing to be commanded and oppressed by the great ones, and the great ones are not to be satisfied without it. From this diversity of appetite one of these three effects do arise—principality, liberty, or licentiousness. Principality is caused either by the people or the great ones, as either the one or the other has occasion; the great ones, finding themselves unable to resist the popular torrent, do many times unanimously confer their whole authority upon one person, and create him prince, that under his protection they may be quiet and secure. The people, on the other side, when overpowered by their adversaries, do the same thing, transmitting their power to a single person, who is made king for their better defence. He who arrives at the sovereignty by the assistance of the great ones preserves it with more difficulty than he who is advanced by the people, because he has about him many of his old associates, who, thinking themselves his equals, are not to be directed and managed as he would have them. But he that is preferred by the people stands alone without equals, and has nobody, or very few, about him but what are ready to obey; moreover, the grandees are hardly to be satisfied without injury to others, which is otherwise with the people, because their designs are more reasonable than the designs of the great ones, which are fixed upon commanding and oppressing altogether, whilst the people endeavour only to defend and secure themselves. Moreover, where the people are adverse the prince can never be safe, by reason of their numbers; whereas the great ones are but few, and by consequence not so dangerous. The worst that a prince can expect from an injured and incensed people is to be deserted; but, if the great ones be provoked, he is not only to fear abandoning, but conspiracy and banding against him; for the greater sort being more provident and cunning, they look out in time to their own safety, and make their interest with the person who they hope will overcome. Besides, the prince is obliged to live always with one and the same people; but with the grandees he is under no such obligation, for he may create and degrade, advance and remove them as he pleases. But for the better explication of this part, I say, that these great men are to be considered two ways especially; that is, whether in the manner of their administration they do wholly follow the fortune and interest of the prince, or whether they do otherwise. Those who devote themselves entirely to his business, and are not rapacious, are to be valued and preferred. Those who are more remiss, and will not stick to their prince, do it commonly upon two motives, either out of laziness or fear (and in those cases they may be employed, especially if they be wise and of good counsel, because, if affairs prosper, thou gainest honour thereby; if they miscarry, thou needest not to fear them) or upon ambition and design, and that is a token that their thoughts are more intent upon their own advantage than thine. Of these a prince ought always to have a more than ordinary care, and order them as if they were enemies professed; for in his distress they will be sure to set him forwards, and do what they can to destroy him. He, therefore, who comes to be prince by the favour and suffrage of the people is obliged to keep them his friends, which (their desire being nothing but freedom from oppression) may be easily done. But he that is preferred by the interest of the nobles against the minds of the commons, is, above all things, to endeavour to ingratiate with the people, which will be as the other if he undertakes their protection; and men receiving good offices, where they expected ill, are endeared by the surprise, and become better affected to their benefactor than perhaps they would have been had he been made prince by their immediate favour.* There are many ways of insinuating† with the people of which no certain rule can be given, because they vary according to the diversity of the subject, and therefore I shall pass them at this time, concluding with this assertion—that it is necessary, above all things, that a prince preserves the affections of his people, otherwise, in any exigence, he has no refuge or remedy. Nabides, Prince of the Spartans, sustained all Greece and a victorious army of the Romans, and defended the government and country against them all; and to do that great action it was sufficient for him to secure himself against the machinations of a few; whereas, if the people had been his enemy, that would not have done it. Let no man impugn my opinion with that old saying, "He that builds upon the people builds upon the sand." That is true, indeed, when a citizen of private condition relies upon the people, and persuades himself that when the magistrate or his adversary goes about to oppress him they will bring him off, in which case many precedents may be produced, and particularly the Gracchi in Rome, and Georgio Scali in Florence. But if the prince that builds upon them knows how to command, and be a man of courage, not dejected in adversity, nor deficient in his other preparations, but keeps up the spirits of his people by his own valour and conduct, he shall never be deserted by them, nor find his foundations laid in a wrong place.

These kind of governments are most tottering and uncertain when the prince strains of a sudden, and passes, as at one leap, from a civil to an absolute power; and the reason is, because they either command and act by themselves or by the ministry and mediation of the magistrate. In this last case their authority is

---

*Editor: The convert is always a greater enthusiast for the cause than one who is born to it.

† Editor: Gaining favour.

weaker and more ticklish,★ because it depends much upon the pleasure and concurrence of the chief officers, who, in time of adversity especially, can remove them easily, either by neglecting or resisting their commands; nor is there any way for such a prince, in the perplexity of his affairs, to establish a tyranny, because those citizens and subjects who used to exercise the magistracy retain still such power and influence upon the people, that they will not infringe the laws to obey his; and in time of danger he shall always want such as he can trust. So that a prince is not to take his measures according to what he sees in times of peace, when of the subjects, having nothing to do but to be governed, every one runs, every one promises, and every one dies for him when death is at a distance; but when times are tempestuous, and the ship of the State has need of the help and assistance of the subject, there are but few will expose themselves, and this experiment is the more dangerous because it can be practised but once. So, then, a prince who is provident and wise ought to carry himself so that in all places, times, and occasions the people may have need of his administration and regiment,† and ever after they shall be faithful and true.

CHAPTER X

How the strength of all Principalities is to be computed.

To any man that examines the nature of principalities, it is worthy his consideration whether a prince has power and territory enough to subsist by himself, or whether he needs the assistance

---

★ *Editor:* Difficult.
† *Editor:* Organization.

and protection of other people. To clear the point a little better, I think those princes capable of ruling who are able, either by the numbers of their men or the greatness of their wealth, to raise a complete army, and bid battle to any that shall invade them; and those I think depend upon others, who of themselves dare not meet their enemy in the field, but are forced to keep within their bounds and defend them as well they can. Of the first we have spoken already, and shall say more as occasion is presented. Of the second no more can be said, but to advise such princes to strengthen and fortify the capital town in their dominions, and not to trouble themselves with the whole country; and whoever shall do that, and in other things manage himself with the subjects as I have described, and perhaps shall do hereafter, shall with great caution be invaded; for men are generally wary and tender of enterprising anything that is difficult, and no great easiness is to be found in attacking a town well fortified and provided, where the prince is not hated by the people.

The towns in Germany are many of them free; though their country and district be but small, yet they obey the Emperor but when they please, and are in no awe either of him or any other prince of the empire, because they are all so well fortified. Every one looks upon the taking of any one of them as a work of great difficulty and time, their walls being so strong, their ditches so deep, their works so regular and well provided with cannon, and their stores and magazines always furnished for a twelve-month. Besides, which, for the aliment and sustenance of the people, and that they may be no burden to the public, they have workhouses where, for a year together, the poor may be employed in such things as are the nerves and life of that city, and sustain themselves by their labour. Military discipline and exercises are likewise in much request there, and many laws and good customs they have to maintain them.

A prince then who has a city well fortified, and the affections of his people, is not easily to be molested, and he that does molest him is like to repent it; for the affairs of this world are so various, it is almost impossible for any army to lie quietly a whole year before a town without interruption. If any objects that the people having houses and possessions out of the town will not have patience to see them plundered and burned, and that charity to themselves will make them forget their prince, I answer, that a wise and dexterous prince will easily evade those difficulties by encouraging his subjects and persuading them, sometimes their troubles will not be long; sometimes inculcating and possessing them with the cruelty of the enemy; and sometimes by correcting and securing himself nimbly of such as appear too turbulent and audacious. Moreover, the usual practice is for the enemy to plunder and set the country on fire at their first coming, whilst every man's spirit is high and fixed upon defence; so that the prince needs not concern himself, nor be fearful of that, for those mischiefs are passed, and inconveniencies received, and when the people in three or four days' time begin to be cool, and consider things soberly, they will find there is no remedy, and join more cordially with the prince, looking upon him as under an obligation to them for having sacrificed their houses and estates in his defence. And the nature of man is such to take as much pleasure in having obliged another as in being obliged himself. Wherefore, all things fairly considered, it is no such hard matter for a prince not only to gain, but to retain, the affection of his subjects, and make them patient of a long siege, if he be wise and provident, and takes care they want nothing either for their livelihood or defence.

CHAPTER XI

Of Ecclesiastical Principalities.

There remains nothing of this nature to be discoursed but of Ecclesiastical Principalities, about which the greatest difficulty is to get into possession, because they are gained either by fortune or virtue, but kept without either, being supported by ancient statutes universally received in the Christian Church, which are of such power and authority they do keep their prince in his dignity, let his conversation or conduct be what it will. These are the only persons who have lands and do not defend them; subjects, and do not govern them; and yet their lands are not taken from them, though they never defend them; nor their subjects dissatisfied, though they never regard them: so that these principalities are the happiest and most secure in the world, by being managed by a supernatural power, above the wisdom and contrivance of man. I shall speak no more of them, for, being set up and continued by God Himself, it would be great presumption in any man who should undertake to dispute them. Nevertheless, if it should be questioned how it came to pass that in temporal things the Church is arrived at that height, seeing that, before Alexander's time, the Italian princes, not only such as were sovereigns, but every baron and lord, how inconsiderable soever in temporal affairs, esteemed of them but little; yet, since it has been able not only to startle and confront the King of France, but to drive him out of Italy, and to ruin the Venetians, the reason of which, though already well known, I think it not superfluous to revive in some measure.

Before Charles, King of France, passed himself into Italy, that province was under the empire of the Pope, the Venetians, the King of Naples, Duke of Milan, and the Florentines. It was the interest of these potentates to have a care, some of them that no foreign prince should come with an army into Italy, and some that none among themselves should usurp upon the other. Those of whom the rest were concerned to be most jealous were the Pope and the Venetians; to restrain the Venetians all the rest were used to confederate, as in the defence of Ferrara. To keep under the Pope, the Roman barons contributed much, who, being divided into two factions (the Ursini and Colonnesi, in perpetual contention, with their arms constantly in their hands under the very nose of the Pope), they kept the pontifical power very low and infirm; and although now and then there happened a courageous Pope, as Sextus, yet neither his courage, wisdom, nor fortune was able to disentangle him from those incommodities, and the shortness of their reign was the reason thereof; for ten years' time, which was as much as any of them reigned, was scarce sufficient for the suppression of either of the parties; and when the Colonnesi, as a man may say, were almost extinct, a new enemy sprang up against the Ursini, which revived the Colonnesi and re-established them again. This emulation and animosity at home was the cause the Pope was no more formidable in Italy. After this, Alexander VI. was advanced to the Papacy, who, more than all that had ever been before him, demonstrated what a Pope with money and power was able to do. Having taken advantage of the French invasion, by the ministry and conduct of Duke Valentine, he performed all that I have mentioned elsewhere among the actions of the said Duke. And though his design was not so much to advantage the Church as to aggrandize the Duke, yet what he did for the one turned afterwards to the benefit of the other; for, the Pope being dead and Valentine extinct, what both of them had got devolved upon the Church. After him Julius succeeded, and found the Church in a flourishing condition. Romagna was wholly in its possession, the barons of Rome exterminated and gone, and their factions suppressed by Pope Alexander, and, besides, a way opened for raising and hoarding of money never practised before; which way Julius improving rather than otherwise, he began to entertain thoughts, not only of conquering Bologna, but mastering the Venetians and forcing the French out of Italy; all which great enterprises succeeding, it added much to his honour that he impropriated nothing, but gave all to the Church. He maintained also the Colonnesi and Ursini in the same condition as he found them; and though in case of sedition there were those ready on both sides to have headed them, yet there were two considerations which kept them at peace: one was the greatness of the Church, which kept them in awe; the other was their want of cardinals, which indeed was the original of their discontent, and will never cease till some of them be advanced to that dignity; for by them the parties in Rome and without are maintained, and the barons obliged to defend them. So that the ambition of the prelates is the cause of all the dissension and tumults among the barons.

His present Holiness Pope Leo had the happiness to be elected at a time when it was most powerful, and it is hoped, if they made the Church great by their arms, he, by the integrity of his conversation and a thousand other virtues, will enlarge it much more, and make it more venerable and august.

CHAPTER XII

How many Forms there are of Military Discipline,
and of those Soldiers which are called Mercenary.

Having spoken particularly of the several sorts of principalities, as I proposed in the beginning; considered in part the reasons of their constitution and their evil, and the ways which many have taken to acquire and preserve them; it remains that I proceed now in a general way upon such things as may conduce to the offence or defence of either of them.

We have declared before that it is not only expedient but necessary for a prince to take care his foundations be good, otherwise his fabric will be sure to fail.

The principal foundations of all States—new, old, or mixed—are good laws and good arms; and because there cannot be good laws where there are not good arms, and where the arms are good there must be good laws, I shall pass by the laws and discourse of the arms.

I say the arms, then, with which a prince defends his State are his own, mercenary, auxiliary, or mixed. The mercenary and auxiliary are unprofitable and dangerous, and that prince who founds the duration of his government upon his mercenary forces shall never be firm or secure; for they are divided, ambitious, undisciplined, unfaithful, insolent to their friends, abject to their enemies, without fear of God or faith to men; so the ruin of that person who trusts to them is no longer protracted than the attempt is deferred; in time of peace they divorce you, in time of war they desert you, and the reason is because it is not love nor any principle of honour that keeps them in the field; it is only their pay, and that is not a consideration strong enough to prevail with them to die for you; whilst you have no service to employ them in, they are excellent soldiers; but tell them of an engagement, and they will either disband before or run away in the battle.

And to evince this would require no great pains; seeing the ruin of Italy proceeded from no other cause than that for several years together it had reposed itself upon mercenary arms, which forces it is possible may have formerly done service to some particular person, and behaved themselves well enough among one another; but no sooner were they attacked by a powerful foreigner, but they discovered themselves, and showed what they were to the world. Hence it was that Charles VII. chalked out his own way into Italy; and that person was in the right who affirmed our own faults were the cause of our miseries. But it was not those faults he believed, but those I have mentioned, which being committed most eminently by princes, they suffered most remarkably in the punishment. But to come closer to the point, and give you a clearer prospect of the imperfection and infelicity of those forces. The great officers of these mercenaries are men of great courage, or otherwise; if the first, you can never be safe, for they always aspire to make themselves great, either by supplanting of you who is their master, or oppressing of other people whom you desired to have preserved; and, on the other side, if the commanders be not courageous, you are ruined again. If it should be urged that all generals will do the same, whether mercenaries or others, I would answer, that all war is managed either by a prince or republic. The prince is obliged to go in person, and perform the office of general himself; the republic must depute some one of her choice citizens, who is to be changed if he carries himself ill; if he behaves himself well he is to be continued, but so straitened and circumscribed by his commission that he may not transgress. And indeed experience tells us that princes alone, and commonwealths alone, with their own private forces have performed great things, whereas mercenaries do nothing but hurt. Besides, a martial commonwealth that stands upon its own legs and maintains itself by its own prowess is not easily usurped, and falls not so readily under the obedience of one of their fellow-citizens as where all the forces are foreign. Rome and Sparta maintained their own liberty for many years together by their own forces and arms. The Swiss are more martial than their neighbours, and by consequence more free. Of the danger of mercenary forces we have an ancient example in the Carthaginians, who, after the end of their first war with the Romans, had like to have been ruined and overrun by their own mercenaries, though their own citizens commanded them.

After the death of Epaminondas the Thebans made Philip of Macedon their general, who defeated their enemies and enslaved themselves. Upon the death of Duke Philip the Milanese entertained Francesco Sforza against the Venetians, and Francesco, having worsted the enemy at Caravaggio, joined himself with him, with design to have mastered his masters. Francesco's father was formerly in the service of Joan, Queen of Naples, and on a sudden marched away from her with his army and left her utterly destitute, so that she was constrained to throw herself under the protection of the King of Arragon; and though the Venetians and Florentines both have lately enlarged their dominion by employing these forces, and their generals have rather advanced than enslaved them, I answer that the Florentines may impute it to their good fortune, because of such of their generals as they might have rationally feared some had no victories to encourage them, others were obstructed, and others turned their ambition another way. He that was not victorious was Giovanni Acuto, whose fidelity could not be known because he had no opportunity to break it, but everybody knows, had he succeeded, the Florentines had been all at his mercy. Sforza had always the Braccheschi in opposition, and they were reciprocally an impediment the one to the other. Francesco turned his ambition upon Lombardy, Braccio upon the Church and the kingdom of Naples. But to speak of more modern occurrences. The Florentines made Paul Vitelli their general, a wise man, and one who from a private fortune had raised himself to a great reputation. Had Paul taken Pisa, nobody can be insensible how the Florentines must have comported with him; for should he have quitted their service and taken pay of their enemy they had been lost without remedy, and to have continued him in that power had been in time to have made him their master. If the progress of the Venetians be considered, they will be found to have acted securely and honourably whilst their affairs were managed by their own forces (which was before they attempted anything upon the *terra firma*); then all was done by the gentlemen and common people of that city, and they did very great things; but when they began to enterprise at land, they began to abate of their old reputation and discipline and to degenerate into the customs of Italy; and when they began to conquer first upon the continent, having no great territory, and their reputation being formidable abroad, there was no occasion that they should be much afraid of their officers; but afterwards, when they began to extend their empire under the command of Carmignola, then it was they became sensible of their error; for having found him to be a great captain by their victories, under his conduct, against the Duke of Milan, perceiving him afterwards grow cool and remiss in their service, they concluded no more great things were to be expected from him; and being neither willing, nor indeed able, to take away his commission, for fear of losing what they had got, they were constrained for their own security to put him to death. Their generals after him were Bartolomeo da Bargamo, Roberto da San Severino, and the Conte de Pitigliano, and such as they, under whose conduct the Venetians were more like to lose than to gain, as it happened not long after at Vaila, where in one battle they lost as much as they had been gaining eight hundred years with incredible labour and difficulty; which is not strange, if it be considered that by those kind of forces the conquests are slow, and tedious, and weak; but their losses are rapid and wonderful.

And because I am come with my examples into Italy, where for many years all things have been managed by mercenary armies, I shall lay my discourse a little higher, that their original and progress being rendered more plain, they may with more ease be regulated and corrected. You must understand that in later times, when the Roman empire began to decline in Italy, and the Pope to take upon him authority in temporal affairs, Italy became divided into several States; for many of the great cities took arms against their nobility, who, having been formerly favoured by the emperors, kept the people under oppression, against which the Church opposed, to gain to itself a reputation and interest in temporal affairs; other cities were subdued by their citizens, who made themselves princes; so that Italy, upon the translation of the empire, being fallen into the hands of the Pope and some other commonwealths, and those priests and citizens unacquainted with the use and exercise of arms, they began to take foreigners into their pay. The first man who gave reputation to these kind of forces was Alberigo da Como of Romagna; among the rest, Braccio and Sforza (the two great arbiters of Italy in their time) were brought up under his discipline, after whom succeeded the rest who commanded the armies in Italy to our days; and the end of their great discipline and conduct was, that Italy was overrun by Charles, pillaged by Louis, violated by Ferrand, and defamed by the Swiss. The order which they observed was, first to take away the reputation from the foot and appropriate it to themselves; and this they did, because their dominion being but small, and to be maintained by their own industry, a few foot could not do their business, and a great body they could not maintain. Hereupon they changed their militia into horse, which, being digested into troops, they sustained and rewarded themselves with the comannds, and by degrees this way of cavalry was grown so much in fashion that in an army of 20,000 men there were scarce 2,000 foot to be found. Besides, they endeavoured with all possible industry to prevent trouble or fear, either to themselves or their soldiers, and their way was by killing nobody in fight, only taking one another prisoners, and dismissing them afterwards without either prejudice or ransom. When they were in leaguer before a town, they shot not rudely amongst them in the night, nor did they in the town disturb them with any sallies in their camp; no approaches or intrenchments were made at unseasonable hours, and nothing of lying in the field when winter came on; and all these things did not happen by any negligence in their officers, but were part of their discipline, and introduced, as is said before, to ease the poor soldier both of labour and danger, by which practices they have brought Italy both into slavery and contempt.

CHAPTER XIII

Of Auxiliaries, Mixed, and Natural Soldiers.

Auxiliaries (which are another sort of unprofitable soldiers) are when some potent prince is called in to your assistance and defence; as was done not long since by Pope Julius, who, in his enterprise of Ferrara, having seen the sad experience of his mercenary army, betook himself to auxiliaries, and capitulated with Ferrand, King of Spain, that he should come with his forces to his relief. These armies may do well enough for themselves, but he who invites them is sure to be a sufferer; for if they be beaten, he is sure to be a loser; if they succeed, he is left at their discretion; and though ancient histories are full of examples of this kind, yet I shall keep to that of Pope Julius XI., as one still fresh in our memory, whose expedition against Ferrara was very rash and inconsiderate, in that he put all into the hands of a stranger; but his good fortune presented him with a third accident, which prevented his reaping the fruit of his imprudent election; for his subsidiary troops being broke at Ravenna, and the Swiss coming in and beating off the victors, beyond all expectation he escaped being a prisoner to his enemies, because they also were defeated, and to his auxiliary friends, because he had conquered by other people's arms. The Florentines, being destitute of soldiers, hired 10,000 French for the reduction of Pisa, by which counsel they ran themselves into greater danger than ever they had done in all their troubles before. The Emperor of Constantinople, in opposition to his neighbours, sent 10,000 Turks into Greece, which could not be got out again when the war was at an end, but gave the first beginning to the servitude and captivity which those infidels brought upon that country. He, then, who has no mind to overcome may make use of these forces, for they are much more dangerous than the mercenary, and will ruin you out of hand, because they are always unanimous, and at the command of other people; whereas the mercenaries, after they have gotten a victory, must have longer time and more occasion before they can do you a mischief, in respect they are not one body, but made up out of several countries entertained into your pay, to which, if you add a general of your own, they cannot suddenly assume so much authority as will be able to do you any prejudice. In short, it is cowardice and sloth that is to be feared in the mercenaries, and courage and activity in the auxiliaries. A wise prince, therefore, never made use of these forces, but committed himself to his own, choosing rather to be overcome with them than to conquer with the other, because he cannot think that a victory which is obtained by other people's arms. I shall make no scruple to produce Cæsar Borgia for an example. This Duke invaded Romagna with an army of auxiliaries, consisting wholly of French, by whose assistance he took Imola and Furli; but finding them afterwards to totter in their faith, and himself insecure, he betook himself to mercenaries as the less dangerous of the two, and entertained the Ursini and Vitelli into his pay; finding them also irresolute, unfaithful, and dangerous, he dismissed them, and for the future employed none but his own. From hence we may collect the difference betwixt these two sorts of forces, if we consider the difference in the Duke's reputation when the Ursini and Vitelli were in his service and when he had no soldiers but his own. When he began to stand upon his own legs his renown began to increase, and, indeed, before his esteem was not so great till everybody found him absolute master of his own army.

Having begun my examples in Italy I am unwilling to leave it, especially whilst it supplies us with such as are fresh in our memory; yet I cannot pass by Hiero of Syracuse, whom I have mentioned before. This person, being made general of the Syracusan army, quickly discovered the mercenary militia was not to be relied upon, their officers being qualified like ours in Italy, and, finding that he could neither continue nor discharge them securely, he ordered things so that they were all cut to pieces, and then prosecuted the war with his own forces alone, without any foreign assistance. To this purpose the Old Testament affords us a figure not altogether improper. When David presented himself to Saul, and offered his service against Goliath, the champion of the Philistines, Saul, to encourage him, accoutred him in his own arms; but David, having tried them on, excused himself, pretending they were unfit, and that with them he should not be able to manage himself; wherefore he desired he might go forth against the enemy with his own arms only, which were his sling and his sword. The sum of all is, the arms of other people are commonly unfit, and either too wide, or too strait, or too cumbersome.

Charles VII., the father of Louis XI., having by his fortune and courage redeemed his country out of the hands of the English, began to understand the necessity of having soldiers of his own, and erected a militia at home, to consist of horse as well as foot, after which his son, King Louis, cashiered his own foot and took the Swiss into his pay, which error being followed by his successors (as is visible to this day) is the occasion of all the dangers to which that kingdom of France is still obnoxious; for, having advanced the reputation of the Swiss, he villified his own people by disbanding the foot entirely, and accustoming his horse so much to engage with other soldiers that, fighting still in conjunction with the Swiss, they began to believe they could do nothing without them; hence it proceeds that the French are not able to do anything against the Swiss, and without them they will venture upon nothing; so that the French army is mixed, consists of mercenaries and natives, and is much better than either mercenaries or auxiliaries alone, but much worse than if it were entirely natural, as this example testifies abundantly; for doubtless France would be insuperable if Charles's establishment was made use of and improved. But the imprudence of man begins many things which, savouring of present good, conceal the poison that is latent, as I said before of the hectic fever; wherefore, if he who is raised to any sovereignty foresees not a mischief till it falls upon his head, he is not to be reckoned a wise prince, and truly that is a particular blessing of God bestowed upon few people. If we reflect upon the first cause of the ruin of the Roman empire, it will be found to begin at their entertaining the Goths into their service, for thereby they weakened and enervated their own native courage, and, as it were, transfused it into them.

I conclude, therefore, that without having proper and peculiar forces of his own, no prince is secure, but depends wholly upon fortune, as having no natural and intrinsic strength to sustain him in adversity; and it was always the opinion and position of wise men, that nothing is so infirm and unstable as the name of power not founded upon forces of its own. Those forces are composed of your subjects, your citizens, or servants; all the rest are either mercenaries or auxiliaries: and as to the manner of ordering and disciplining these domestics, it will not be hard if the orders which I have prescribed be perused, and the way considered which Philip the father of Alexander the Great, and many other princes and republics, have used in the like cases, to which orders and establishments I do wholly refer you.

CHAPTER XIV

The Duty of a Prince in relation to his Militia.

A prince, then, is to have no other design, nor thought, nor study but war and the arts and disciplines of it; for, indeed, that is the only profession worthy of a prince, and is of so much importance that it not only preserves those who are born princes in their patrimonies, but advances men of private condition to that honourable degree. On the other side, it is frequently seen, when princes have addicted themselves more to delicacy and softness than to arms, they have lost all, and been driven out of their States; for the principal thing which deprives or gains a man authority is the neglect or profession of that art. Francesco Sforza, by his experience in war, of a private person made himself Duke of Milan, and his children, seeking to avoid the fatigues and incommodities thereof, of dukes became private men;

for, among other evils and inconveniences which attend when you are ignorant in war, it makes you contemptible, which is a scandal a prince ought with all diligence to avoid, for reasons I shall name hereafter; besides, betwixt a potent and an impotent, a vigilant and a negligent prince, there is no proportion, it being unreasonable that a martial and generous person should be subject willingly to one that is weak and remiss, or that those who are careless and effeminate should be safe amongst those who are military and active; for the one is too insolent and the other too captious ever to do anything well together: so that a prince unacquainted with the discipline of war, besides other infelicities to which he is exposed, cannot be beloved by, nor confident in, his armies. He never, therefore, ought to relax his thoughts from the exercises of war not so much as in time of peace; and, indeed, then he should employ his thoughts more studiously therein than in war itself, which may be done two ways, by the application of the body and the mind. As to his bodily application, or matter of action, besides that he is obliged to keep his armies in good discipline and exercise, he ought to inure himself to sports, and by hunting and hawking, and such like recreation, accustom his body to hardship, and hunger, and thirst, and at the same time inform himself of the coasts and situation of the country, the bigness and elevation of the mountains, the largeness and avenues of the valleys, the extent of the plains, the nature of the rivers and fens, which is to be done with great curiosity; and this knowledge is useful two ways, for hereby he not only learns to know his own country and to provide better for its defence, but it prepares and adapts him, by observing their situations, to comprehend the situation of other countries, which will perhaps be necessary for him to discover; for the hills, the vales, the plains, the rivers, and the marshes (for example, in Tuscany), have a certain similitude and resemblance with those in other provinces; so that, by the knowledge of one, we may easily imagine the rest; and that prince who is defective in this, wants the most necessary qualification of a general; for by knowing the country, he knows how to beat up his enemy, take up his quarters, march his armies, draw up his men, and besiege a town with advantage. In the character which historians give of Philopomenes, Prince of Achaia, one of his great commendations is, that in time of peace he thought of nothing but military affairs, and when he was in company with his friends in the country, he would many times stop suddenly and expostulate with them: If the enemy were upon that hill, and our army where we are, which would have the advantage of the ground? How could we come at them with most security? If we would draw off, how might we do it best? Or, if they would retreat, how might we follow? So that as he was travelling, he would propose all the accidents to which an army was subject; he would hear their opinion, give them his own, and reinforce it with arguments; and this he did so frequently, that by continual practice and a constant intention of his thoughts upon that business, he brought himself to that perfection, no accident could happen, no inconvenience could occur to an army, but he could presently redress it. But as to the exercise of the mind, a prince is to do that by diligence in history and solemn consideration of the actions of the most excellent men, by observing how they demeaned themselves in the wars, examining the grounds and reasons of their victories and losses, that he may be able to avoid the one and imitate the other; and above all, to keep close to the example of some great captain of old (if any such occurs in his reading), and not only to make him his pattern, but to have all his actions perpetually in his mind, as it was said Alexander did by Achilles, Cæsar by Alexander, Scipio by Cyrus. And whoever reads the life of Cyrus, written by Xenophon, will find how much Scipio advantaged his renown by that imitation, and how much in modesty, affability, humanity, and liberality he framed himself to the description which Xenophon had given him. A wise prince, therefore, is to observe all these rules, and never be idle in time of peace, but employ himself therein with all his industry, that in his adversity he may reap the fruit of it, and when fortune frowns, be ready to defy her.

CHAPTER XV

Of such things as render Men (especially Princes)
worthy of Blame or Applause.

It remains now that we see in what manner a prince ought to comport with his subjects and friends; and because many have written of this subject before, it may perhaps seem arrogant in me, especially considering that in my discourse I shall deviate from the opinion of other men. But my intention being to write for the benefit and advantage of him who understands, I thought it more convenient to respect the essential verity than the imagination of the thing (and many have framed imaginary commonwealths and governments to themselves which never were seen nor had any real existence), for the present manner of living is so different from the way that ought to be taken, that he who neglects what is done to follow what ought to be done, will sooner learn how to ruin than how to preserve himself; for a tender man, and one that desires to be honest in everything, must needs run a great hazard among so many of a contrary principle. Wherefore it is necessary for a prince who is willing to subsist to harden himself, and learn to be good or otherwise according to the exigence of his affairs. Laying aside, therefore, all imaginable notions of a prince, and discoursing of nothing but what is actually true, I say that all men when they are spoken of, especially princes, who are in a higher and more eminent station, are remarkable for some quality or other that makes them either honourable or contemptible. Hence it is that some are counted liberal, others miserable (according to the propriety of the Tuscan word *Misero,* for *Quaro* in our language is one that desires to acquire by rapine or any other way; *Misero* is he that abstains too much from making use of his own),★ some munificent, others rapacious; some cruel, others merciful; some faithless, others precise; one poor-spirited and effeminate, another fierce and ambitious; one courteous, another haughty; one modest, another libidinous; one sincere, another cunning; one rugged and morose, another accessible and easy; one grave, another giddy; one a devout, another an atheist. No man, I am sure, will deny but that it would be an admirable thing and highly to be commended to have a prince endued with all the good qualities aforesaid; but because it is impossible to have, much less to exercise, them all by reason of the frailty and crossness of our nature, it is convenient that he be so well instructed as to know how to avoid the scandal of those vices which may deprive him of his state, and be very cautious of the rest, though their consequence be not so pernicious, but where they are unavoidable he need trouble himself the less. Again, he is not to concern himself if run under the infamy of those vices without which his dominion was not to be preserved; for if we consider things impartially we shall find some things in appearance are virtuous, and yet, if pursued, would bring certain destruction; and others, on the contrary, that are seemingly bad, which, if followed by a prince, procure his peace and security.

★ *Editor:* Hence the word "miser" in English.

CHAPTER XVI

Of Liberality and Parsimony.

To begin, then, with the first of the above-mentioned qualities, I say, it would be advantageous to be accounted liberal;
nevertheless, liberality so used as not to render you formidable
does but injure you; for if it be used virtuously and as it ought
to be, it will not be known, nor secure you from the imputation of its contrary. To keep up, therefore, the name of liberal
amongst men, it is necessary that no kind of luxury be omitted,
so that a prince of that disposition will consume his revenue in
those kind of expenses, and he be obliged at last, if he would
preserve that reputation, to become grievous, and a great exac-
tor upon the people, and do whatever is practicable for the getting of money, which will cause him to be hated of his subjects
and despised by everybody else when he once comes to be
poor; so that offending many with his liberality and rewarding
but few, he becomes sensible of the first disaster, and runs great
hazard of being ruined the first time he is in danger; which,
when afterwards he discovers, and desires to remedy, he runs
into the other extreme, and grows as odious for his avarice. So,
then, if a prince cannot exercise this virtue of liberality so as to
be publicly known, without detriment to himself, he ought, if
he be wise, not to dread the imputation of being covetous, for
in time he shall be esteemed liberal when it is discovered that
by his parsimony he has increased his revenue to a condition of
defending him against any invasion, and to enterprise upon
other people without oppressing of them; so that he shall be accounted noble to all from whom he takes nothing away, which
are an infinite number, and near and parsimonious only to such
few as he gives nothing to.

In our days we have seen no great action done but by those who were accounted miserable, the other have been always undone. Pope Julius XI. made use of his bounty to get into the Chair, but, to enable himself to make war with the King of France, he never practised it after, and by his frugality he maintained several wars without any tax or imposition upon the people, his long parsimony having furnished him for his extraordinary expenses. The present King of Spain, if he had affected to be thought liberal, could never have undertaken so many great designs nor obtained so many great victories. A prince, therefore, ought not so much to concern himself (so he exacts not upon his subjects, so he be able to defend himself, so he becomes not poor and despicable, nor commits rapine upon his people) though he be accounted covetous, for that is one of those vices which fortifies his dominion. If any one objects that Cæsar by his liberality made his way to the empire, and many others upon the same score of reputation have made themselves great, I answer, that you are actually a prince, or in a fair way to be made one. In the first case, liberality is hurtful; in the second, it is necessary, and Cæsar was one of those who designed upon the empire. But when he was arrived at that dignity, if he had lived, and not retrenched his expenses, he would have ruined that empire. If any replies, many have been princes, and with their armies performed great matters, who have been reputed liberal, I rejoin that a prince spends either of his own, or his subjects', or other people's. In the first case he is to be frugal; in the second, he may be as profuse as he pleases, and baulk no point of liberality. But that prince whose army is to be maintained with free quarter and plunder and exactions from other people, is obliged to be liberal, or his army will desert him; and well he may be prodigal of what neither belongs to him nor his subjects, as was the case with Cæsar, and Cyrus, and Alexander;

for to spend upon another's stock rather adds to than subtracts from his reputation; it is spending of his own that is so mortal and pernicious. Nor is there anything that destroys itself like liberality; for in the use of it, taking away the faculty of using it, thou becomest poor and contemptible, or, to avoid that poverty, thou makest thyself odious and a tyrant; and there is nothing of so much importance to a prince to prevent as to be either contemptible or odious, both which depend much upon the prudent exercise of your liberality. Upon these considerations it is more wisdom to lie under the scandal of being miserable, which is an imputation rather infamous than odious, than to be thought liberal and run yourself into a necessity of playing the tyrant, which is infamous and odious both.

CHAPTER XVII

Of Cruelty and Clemency, and whether it is best for a Prince to be beloved or feared.

To come now to the other qualities proposed, I say every prince is to desire to be esteemed rather merciful than cruel, but with great caution that his mercy be not abused; Cæsar Borgia was counted cruel, yet that cruelty reduced Romagna, united it, settled it in peace, and rendered it faithful; so that if well considered, he will appear much more merciful than the Florentines, who rather than be thought cruel suffered Pistoia to be destroyed. A prince, therefore, is not to regard the scandal of being cruel, if thereby he keeps his subjects in their allegiance and united, seeing by some few examples of justice you may be more merciful than they who by an universal exercise of pity permit several disorders to follow, which occasion rapine and murder; and the reason is, because that exorbitant mercy has an ill effect upon the whole universality, whereas particular executions extend only to particular persons. But among all princes a new prince has the hardest task to avoid the scandal of being cruel by reason of the newness of his government, and the dangers which attend it: hence Virgil in the person of Dido excused the inhospitality of her government.

> *Res dura, & regni novitas, me talia cogunt*
> *Moliri, & late fines Custode tueri.*

> My new dominion and my harder fate
> Constrains me to't, and I must guard my State.

Nevertheless, he is not to be too credulous of reports, too hasty in his motions, nor create fears and jealousies to himself, but so to temper his administrations with prudence and humanity that neither too much confidence may make him careless, nor too much diffidence intolerable. And from hence arises a new question, Whether it be better to be beloved than feared, or feared than beloved? It is answered, both would be convenient, but because that is hard to attain, it is better and more secure, if one must be wanting, to be feared than beloved; for in the general men are ungrateful, inconstant, hypocritical, fearful of danger, and covetous of gain; whilst they receive any benefit by you, and the danger is at a distance, they are absolutely yours, their blood, their estates, their lives and their children, as I said before, are all at your service; but when mischief is at hand, and you have present need of their help, they make no scruple to revolt; and that prince who leaves himself naked of other preparations, and relies wholly upon their professions, is sure to be ruined; for amity contracted by price, and not by the greatness and generosity of the mind, may seem a good penny-worth; yet when you have occasion to make use of it, you will find no such thing. Moreover, men do with less remorse offend against those who desire to be beloved than against those who are ambitious of being feared, and the reason is because love is fastened only by a ligament of obligation, which the ill-nature of mankind breaks upon every occasion that is presented to his profit; but fear depends upon an apprehension of punishment, which is never to be dispelled. Yet a prince is to render himself awful in such sort that, if he gains not his subjects' love, he may eschew their hatred; for to be feared and not hated are compatible enough, and he may be always in that condition if he offers no violence to their estates, nor attempts anything upon the honour of their wives, as also when he has occasion to take away any man's life, if he takes his time when the cause is manifest, and he has good matter for his justification; but above all things he is to have a care of intrenching upon their estates, for men do sooner forget the death of their father than the loss of their patrimony; besides, occasions of confiscation never fail, and he that once gives way to that humour of rapine shall never want temptation to ruin his neighbour. But, on the contrary, provocations to blood are more rare, and do sooner evaporate; but when a prince is at the head of his army, and has a multitude of soldiers to govern, then it is absolutely necessary not to value the epithet of cruel, for without that no army can be kept in unity, nor in disposition for any great act.

Among the several instances of Hannibal's great conduct, it is one that, having a vast army constituted out of several nations, and conducted to make war in an enemy's country, there never happened any sedition among them, or any mutiny against their general, either in his adversity or prosperity: which can proceed from nothing so probably as his great cruelty, which, added to his infinite virtues, rendered him both awful and terrible to his soldiers, and without that all his virtues would have signified nothing. Some writers there are, but of little consideration, who admire his great exploits and condemn the true causes of them. But to prove that his other virtues would never have carried him through, let us reflect upon Scipio, a person honourable not only in his own time, but in all history whatever; nevertheless his army mutinied in Spain, and the true cause of it was his too much gentleness and lenity, which gave his soldiers more liberty than was suitable or consistent with military discipline. Fabius Maximus upbraided him by it in the Senate, and called him corrupter of the Roman Militia; the inhabitants of Locris having been plundered and destroyed by one of Scipio's lieutenants, they were never redressed, nor the legate's insolence corrected, all proceeding from the mildness of Scipio's nature, which was so eminent in him, that a person undertaking to excuse him in the Senate, declared that there were many who knew better how to avoid doing ill themselves than to punish it in other people; which temper would doubtless in time have eclipsed the glory and reputation of Scipio, had that authority been continued in him; but receiving orders and living under the direction of the Senate, that ill quality was not only not discovered in him, but turned to his renown. I conclude, therefore, according to what I have said about being feared or beloved, that forasmuch as men do love at their own discretion, but fear at their prince's, a wise prince is obliged to lay his foundation upon that which is in his own power, not that which depends on other people, but, as I said before, with great caution that he does not make himself odious.

CHAPTER XVIII

How far a Prince is obliged by his Promise.

How honourable it is for a prince to keep his word, and act rather with integrity than collusion, I suppose everybody understands: nevertheless, experience has shown in our times that those princes who have not pinned themselves up to that punctuality and preciseness have done great things, and by their cunning and subtilty not only circumvented, and darted the brains of those with whom they had to deal, but have overcome and been too hard for those who have been so superstitiously exact. For further explanation you must understand there are two ways of contending, by law and by force: the first is proper to men; the second to beasts; but because many times the first is insufficient, recourse must be had to the second. It belongs, therefore, to a prince to understand both, when to make use of the rational and when of the brutal way; and this is recommended to princes, though abstrusely, by ancient writers, who tell them how Achilles and several other princes were committed to the education of Chiron the Centaur, who was to keep them under his discipline, choosing them a master, half man and half beast, for no other reason but to show how necessary it is for a prince to be acquainted with both, for that one without the other will be of little duration. Seeing, therefore, it is of such importance to a prince to take upon him the nature and disposition of a beast, of all the whole flock he ought to imitate the lion and the fox; for the lion is in danger of toils and snares, and the fox of the wolf; so that he must be a fox to find out the snares, and a lion to fright away the wolves, but they who keep wholly to the lion have no true notion of themselves. A prince, therefore, who is wise and prudent, cannot or ought not to keep his parole, when the keeping of it is to his prejudice, and the causes for which he promised removed. Were men all good this doctrine was not to be taught, but because they are wicked and not likely to be punctual with you, you are not obliged to any such strictness with them; nor was there ever any prince that wanted lawful pretence to justify his breach of promise. I might instance in many modern examples, and show how many confederations, and peaces, and promises have been broken by the infidelity of princes, and how he that best personated the fox had the better success. Nevertheless, it is of great consequence to disguise your inclination, and to play the hypocrite well; and men are so simple in their temper and so submissive to their present necessities, that he that is neat and cleanly in his collusions shall never want people to practise them upon. I cannot forbear one example which is still fresh in our memory. Alexander VI. never did, nor thought of, anything but cheating, and never wanted matter to work upon; and though no man promised a thing with greater asseveration, nor confirmed it with more oaths and imprecations, and observed them less, yet understanding the world well he never miscarried.

A prince, therefore, is not obliged to have all the forementioned good qualities in reality, but it is necessary he have them in appearance; nay, I will be bold to affirm that, having them actually, and employing them upon all occasions, they are extremely prejudicial, whereas, having them only in appearance, they turn to better account; it is honourable to seem mild, and merciful, and courteous, and religious, and sincere, and indeed to be so, provided your mind be so rectified and prepared that you can act quite contrary upon occasion. And this must be premised, that a prince, especially if come but lately to the throne, cannot observe all those things exactly which make men be esteemed virtuous, being oftentimes necessitated, for the preservation of his State, to do things inhuman, uncharitable, and irreligious; and, therefore, it is convenient his mind be at his command, and flexible to all the puffs and variations of fortune; not forbearing to be good whilst it is in his choice, but knowing how to be evil when there is a necessity. A prince, then, is to have particular care that nothing falls from his mouth but what is full of the five qualities aforesaid, and that to see and to hear him he appears all goodness, integrity, humanity, and religion, which last he ought to pretend to more than ordinarily, because more men do judge by the eye than by the touch; for everybody sees but few understand; everybody sees how you appear, but few know what in reality you are, and those few dare not oppose the opinion of the multitude, who have the majesty of their prince to defend them; and in the actions of all men, especially princes, where no man has power to judge, every one looks to the end. Let a prince, therefore, do what he can to preserve his life, and continue his supremacy, the means which he uses shall be thought honourable, and be commended by everybody; because the people are always taken with the appearance and event of things, and the greatest part of the world consists of the people; those few who are wise taking place when the multitude has nothing else to rely upon. There is a prince at this time in being (but his name I shall conceal) who has nothing in his mouth but fidelity and peace; and yet had he exercised either the one or the other, they had robbed him before this both of his power and reputation.

CHAPTER XIX

*That Princes ought to be cautious of
becoming either odious or contemptible.*

And because in our discourse of the qualifications of a prince we
have hitherto spoken only of those which are of greatest importance, we shall now speak briefly of the rest under these general
heads. That a prince make it his business (as is partly hinted before) to avoid such things as may make him odious or contemptible, and as often as he does that he plays his part very
well, and shall meet no danger or inconveniences by the rest of
his vices. Nothing, as I said before, makes a prince so insuffer-
ably odious as usurping his subjects' estates and debauching their
wives, which are two things he ought studiously to forbear; for
whilst the generality of the world live quietly upon their estates
and unprejudiced in their honour, they live peaceably enough,
and all his contention is only with the pride and ambition of
some few persons who are many ways and with great ease to be
restrained. But a prince is contemptible when he is counted effeminate, light, inconstant, pusillanimous, and irresolute; and of
this he ought to be as careful as of a rock in the sea, and strive
that in all his actions there may appear magnanimity, courage,
gravity, and fortitude, desiring that in the private affairs of his
subjects his sentence and determination may be irrevocable,
and himself to stand so in their opinion that none may think it
possible either to delude or divert him. The prince who causes
himself to be esteemed in that manner shall be highly redoubted,
and if he be feared, people will not easily conspire against him,
nor readily invade him, because he is known to be an excellent
person and formidable to his subjects; for a prince ought to be

terrible in two places—at home to his subjects, and abroad to
his equals, from whom he defends himself by good arms and
good allies; for, if his power be good, his friends will not be
wanting, and while his affairs are fixed at home, there will be
no danger from abroad, unless they be disturbed by some former conspiracy; and upon any commotion *ab extra,* if he be
composed at home, has lived as I prescribe, and not deserted
himself, he will be able to bear up against any impression, according to the example of Nabis the Spartan. When things are
well abroad his affairs at home will be safe enough, unless they
be perplexed by some secret conspiracy, against which the
prince sufficiently provides if he keeps himself from being hated
or despised, and the people remain satisfied of him, which is a
thing very necessary, as I have largely inculcated before. And
one of the best remedies a prince can use against conspiracy is to
keep himself from being hated or despised by the multitude; for
nobody plots but expects by the death of the prince to gratify
the people, and the thought of offending them will deter him
from any such enterprise, because in conspiracies the difficulties
are infinite. By experience we find that many conjurations have
been on foot, but few have succeeded, because no man can conspire alone, nor choose a confederate but out of those who are
discontented; and no sooner shall you impart your mind to a
malcontent but you give him opportunity to reconcile himself,
because there is nothing he proposes to himself but he may
expect from the discovery. So that the gain being certain on that
side, and hazardous and uncertain on the other, he must be
either an extraordinary friend to you or an implacable enemy to
the prince if he does not betray you; in short, on the side of the
conspirators there is nothing but fear and jealousy, and apprehension of punishment; but, on the prince's side, there is the

majesty of the Government, the laws, the assistance of his friends and State, which defend him so effectually that, if the affections of the people be added to them, no man can be so rash and precipitate as to conspire; for if, before the execution of his design, the conspirator has reason to be afraid, in this case he has much more afterwards, having offended the people in the execution and left himself no refuge to fly to. Of this many examples may be produced, but I shall content myself with one which happened in the memory of our fathers. Hanibal Bentivogli, grandfather to this present Hanibal, was Prince of Bolonia, and killed by the Canneschi who conspired against him, none of his race being left behind but John, who was then in his cradle; the murder was no sooner committed but the people took arms and slew all the Canneschi, which proceeded only from the affection that the house of the Bentivogli had at that time among the populace in Bolonia, which was then so great that when Hanibal was dead, there being none of that family remaining in a capacity for the government of the State, upon information that at Florence there was a natural son of the said Bentivogli's, who till that time had passed only for the son of a smith, they sent ambassadors for him, and having conducted him honourably to that city, they gave him the Government, which he executed very well till the said John came of age. I conclude, therefore, a prince need not be much apprehensive of conspiracies whilst the people are his friends; but when they are dissatisfied, and have taken prejudice against him, there is nothing nor no person which he ought not to fear. And it has been the constant care of all wise princes and all well-governed States not to reduce the nobility to despair nor the people to discontent, which is one of the most material things a prince is to prevent. Among the best-ordered monarchies of our times France is one, in which there are many good laws and constitutions tending to the liberty and preservation of the king. The first of them is the Parliament and the authority wherewith it is vested; for he who was the founder of that monarchy, being sensible of the ambition and insolence of the nobles, and judging it convenient to have them bridled and restrained: and knowing, on the other side, the hatred of the people against the nobility, and that it proceeded from fear, being willing to secure them, to exempt the king from the displeasure of the nobles if he sided with the Commons, or from the malice of the Commons if he inclined to the nobles, he erected a third judge, which, without any reflection upon the king, should keep the nobility under, and protect the people; nor could there be a better order, wiser nor of greater security to the king and the kingdom, from whence we may deduce another observation—That princes are to leave things of injustice and envy to the ministry and execution of others, but acts of favour and grace are to be performed by themselves. To conclude, a prince is to value his grandees, but so as not to make the people hate him.

Contemplating the lives and deaths of several of the Roman emperors, it is possible many would think to find plenty of examples quite contrary to my opinion, forasmuch as some of them whose conduct was remarkable, and magnanimity obvious to everybody, were turned out of their authority, or murdered by the conspiracy of their subjects. To give a punctual answer, I should inquire into the qualities and conversations of the said emperors, and in so doing I should find the reason of their ruin to be the same, or very consonant to what I have opposed. And in part I will represent such things as are most notable to the consideration of him that reads the actions of our times, and I shall content myself with the examples of all the emperors which succeeded in the empire from Marcus the philosopher to Maximinus, and they were Marcus, his son Commodus, Pertinax, Julian, Severus,

Antoninus, his son Caracalla, Macrinus, Heliogabalus, Alexander, and Maximinus.

It is first to be considered that, whereas in other Governments there was nothing to contend with but the ambition of the nobles and the insolence of the people, the Roman emperors had a third inconvenience to support against the avarice and cruelty of the soldiers, which was a thing of such difficult practice that it was the occasion of the destruction of many of them, it being very uneasy to please the subject and the soldier together; for the subject loves peace, and chooses therefore a prince that is gentle and mild; whereas the soldier prefers a martial prince, and one that is haughty, and rigid, and rapacious, which good qualities they are desirous he should exercise upon the people, that their pay might be increased, and their covetousness and cruelty satiated upon them. Hence it is, that those emperors who neither by art nor nature are endued with that address and reputation as is necessary for the restraining both of the one and the other, do always miscarry; and of them the greatest part, especially if but lately advanced to the empire, understanding the inconsistency of their two humours, incline to satisfy the soldiers, without regarding how far the people are disobliged; which council is no more than is necessary; for seeing it cannot be avoided but princes must fall under the hatred of somebody, they ought diligently to contend that it be not of the multitude; if that be not to be obtained, their next great care is to be that they incur not the odium of such as are most potent among them. And, therefore, those emperors who were new, and had need of extraordinary support, adhered more readily to the soldiers than to the people, which turned to their detriment or advantage, as the prince knew how to preserve his reputation with them. From the causes aforesaid, it happened that Marcus Aurelius, Pertinax, and Alexander, being princes of more than ordinary modesty, lovers of justice, enemies of cruelty, courteous and bountiful, came all of them (except Marcus) to unfortunate ends. Marcus, indeed, lived and died in great honour, because he came to the empire by way of inheritance and succession, without being beholden either to soldiers or people, and being afterwards endued with many good qualities which recommended him, and made him venerable among them, he kept them both in such order whilst he lived, and held them so strictly to their bounds, that he was never either hated or despised. But Pertinax was chosen emperor against the will of the soldiers, who being used to live licentiously under Commodus, they could not brook that regularity to which Pertinax endeavoured to bring them; so that having contracted the odium of the soldiers, and a certain disrespect and neglect by reason of his age, he was ruined in the very beginning of his reign; from whence it is observable that hatred is obtained two ways, by good works and bad; and, therefore, a prince, as I said before, being willing to retain his jurisdiction, is oftentimes compelled to be bad. For if the chief party, whether it be people, or army, or nobility, which you think most useful and of most consequence to you for the conservation of your dignity, be corrupt, you must follow their humour and indulge them, and in that case honesty and virtue are pernicious.

But let us come to Alexander, who was a prince of such great equity and goodness, it is reckoned among his praises that in the fourteen years of his empire there was no man put to death without a fair trial; nevertheless, being accounted effeminate, and one that suffered himself to be managed by his mother, and falling by that means into disgrace, the army conspired and killed him. Examining, on the other side, the conduct of Commodus, Severus, Antoninus, Caracalla, and Maximinus, you will find them cruel and rapacious, and such as to satisfy the soldiers, omitted no kind of injury that could be exercised against the people, and all of them but Severus were unfortunate in their ends; for Severus was a prince of so great courage and magnanimity, that preserving the friendship of the army, though the people were oppressed, he made his whole reign happy, his virtues having represented him so admirable both to the soldiers and people, that these remained in a manner stupid and astonished, and the other obedient and contented. And because the actions of Severus were great in a new prince, I shall show in brief how he personated the fox and the lion, whose natures and properties are, as I said before, necessary for the imitation of a prince. Severus, therefore, knowing the laziness and inactivity of Julian the emperor, persuaded the army under his command in Sclavonia to go to Rome and revenge the death of Pertinax, who was murdered by the Imperial Guards; and under that colour, without the least pretence to the empire, he marched his army towards Rome, and was in Italy before anything of his motion was known. Being arrived at Rome, the Senate were afraid of him, killed Julian, and elected Severus. After which beginning there remained two difficulties to be removed before he could be master of the whole empire; the one was in Asia, where Niger, General of the Asiatic army, had proclaimed himself emperor; the other in the West, where Albinus the General aspired to the same. And thinking it hazardous to declare against both, he resolved to oppose himself against Niger, and cajole and wheedle Albinus, to whom he wrote word: That being chosen emperor by the Senate, he was willing to receive him to a participation of that dignity, gave him the title of Cæsar, and by consent of the Senate admitted him his colleague, which Albinus embraced very willingly, and thought him in earnest; but when Severus had overcome Niger, put him to death, and settled the affairs of the East, being returned to Rome, he complained in the Senate against Albinus as a person who, contrary to his obligations for the benefits received from him, had endeavoured treacherously to murder him; told them that he was obliged to march against him to punish his ingratitude, and afterwards following him into France, he executed his design, deprived him of his command, and put him to death. He, then, who strictly examines the actions of this prince will find him fierce as a lion, subtile as a fox, feared and reverenced by everybody, and no way odious to his army. Nor will it seem strange that he, though newly advanced to the empire, was able to defend it, seeing his great reputation protected him against the hatred which his people might have conceived against him by reason of his rapine. But his son Antoninus was an excellent person likewise endued with transcendent parts, which rendered him admirable to the people and grateful to the soldiers; for he was martial in his nature, patient of labour and hardship, and a great despiser of all sensuality and softness, which recommended him highly to his armies. Nevertheless, his fury and cruelty was so immoderately great, having upon several private and particular occasions put a great part of the people of Rome, and all the inhabitants of Alexandria, to death, that he fell into the hatred of the whole world, and began to be feared by his confidents that were about him; so that he was killed by one of his captains in the middle of his camp. From whence it may be observed, that these kind of assassinations which follow upon a deliberate and obstinate resolution, cannot be prevented by a prince; for he who values not his own life can commit them when he pleases; but they are to be feared the less, because they happen but seldom, he is only to have a care of doing any great injury to those that are about him, of which error Antoninus was too guilty, having put the brother of the said captain to an ignominious death, threatened the captain daily, and yet continued him in his guards, which was a rash and pernicious act, and proved so in the end. But to come to Commodus, who had no hard task to preserve his empire, succeeding to it by way of inheritance, as son to Marcus, for that to satisfy the people and oblige the soldiers, he had no more to do but to follow the footsteps of his father. But being of a brutish and cruel disposition, to exercise his rapacity upon the people he indulged his army, and allowed them in all manner of licentiousness. Besides prostituting his dignity by descending many times upon the theatre to fight with the gladiators, and committing many other acts which were vile and unworthy the majesty of an emperor, he became contemptible to the soldiers, and growing odious to one party and despicable to the other, they conspired and murdered him. Maximinus was likewise a martial prince, and addicted to the wars, and the army being weary of the effeminacy of Alexander, whom I have mentioned before, having slain him, they made Maximinus emperor, but he possessed it not long; for two things contributed to make him odious and despised. One was the meanness of his extraction, having kept sheep formerly in Thrace, which was known to all the world, and made him universally contemptible; the other was, that at his first coming to the empire, by not repairing immediately to Rome and putting himself into possession of his imperial seat, he had contracted the imputation of being cruel, having exercised more than ordinary severity by his prefects in Rome, and his lieutenants in all the rest of the empire; so that the whole world being provoked by the vileness of his birth and detestation of his cruelty, in apprehension of his fury, Africa, the Senate, and all the people both in Italy and Rome, conspired against him, and his own army joining themselves with them in their leaguer before Aquileia finding it difficult to be taken, weary of his cruelties, and encouraged by the multitude of his enemies, they set upon him and slew him.

I will not trouble myself with Heliogabalus, Macrinus, or Julian, who, being all effeminate and contemptible, were quickly extinguished. But I shall conclude this discourse, and say that the princes of our times are not obliged to satisfy the soldiers in their respective governments by such extraordinary ways; for though they are not altogether to be neglected, yet the remedy and resolution is easy, because none of these princes have entire armies, brought up, and inveterated in their several governments and provinces, as the armies under the Roman empire were. If, therefore, at that time it was necessary to satisfy the soldiers rather than the people, it was because the soldiers were more potent. At present it is more the interest of all princes (except the Great Turk and the Soldan) to comply with the people, because they are more considerable than the soldiers. I except the Turk, because he has in his Guards 12,000 foot and 15,000 horse constantly about him, upon whom the strength and security of his empire depends, and it is necessary (postponing all other respect to the people) they be continued his friends. It is the same case with the Soldan, who, being wholly in the power of the soldiers, it is convenient that he also waive the people and insinuate* with the army. And here it is to be noted that this government of the Soldans is different from all other monarchies, for it is not unlike the Papacy in Christendom, which can neither be called a new nor an hereditary principality, because the children of the deceased prince are neither heirs to his estate nor lords of his empire, but he who is chosen to succeed by those who have the faculty of election; which custom, being of old, the government cannot be called new, and by consequence is not subject to any of the difficulties wherewith a new one is infested; because, though the person of the prince be new, and

---

* *Editor:* Become as one with the army by subtle means.

perhaps the title, yet the laws and orders of State are old, and disposed to receive him as if he were hereditary lord. But to return to our business: I say that whoever considers the aforesaid discourse shall find either hatred or contempt the perpetual cause of the ruin of those emperors, and be able to judge how it came about that, part of them taking one way in their administrations and part of them another, in both parties some where happy, and some unhappy at last. Pertinax and Alexander, being but upstart princes, it was not only vain but dangerous for them to imitate Marcus, who was emperor by right of succession. Again, it was no less pernicious for Caracalla, Commodus, and Maximinus to make Severus their pattern, not having force or virtue enough to follow his footsteps. So, then, if a new prince cannot imitate the actions of Marcus, and to regulate by the example of Severus is unnecessary, he is only to take that part from Severus that is necessary to the foundation of his State, and from Marcus what is convenient to keep and defend it gloriously when it is once established and firm.

CHAPTER XX

Whether Citadels, and other things which Princes
many times do, be profitable or dangerous.

Some princes, for the greater security of their dominion, have disarmed their subjects; others have cantonized their countries; others have fomented factions and animosities among them; some have applied themselves to flatter and insinuate★ with those who were suspicious in the beginning of their government; some have

---

★ *Editor:* Become as one with their subjects who were suspicious of them.

built castles, others have demolished them; and though in all these cases no certain or determined rule can be prescribed, unless we come to a particular consideration of the State where it is to be used, yet I shall speak of them all, as the matter itself will endure. A wise prince, therefore, was never known to disarm his subjects; rather, finding them unfurnished, he put arms into their hands, for by arming them and inuring them to warlike exercise, those arms are surely your own: they who were suspicious to you become faithful; they who are faithful are confirmed, and all your subjects become of your party; and because the whole multitude which submits to your government is not capable of being armed, if you be beneficial and obliging to those you do arm you may make the bolder with the rest, for the difference of your behaviour to the soldier binds him more firmly to your service; and the rest will excuse you, as judging them most worthy of reward who are most liable to danger. But when you disarm you disgust them, and imply a diffidence in them, either for cowardice or treachery, and the one or the other is sufficient to give them an impression of hatred against you. And because you cannot subsist without soldiers, you will be forced to entertain mercenaries, whom I have formerly described; and if it were possible for the said mercenaries to be good, they could not be able to defend you against powerful adversaries and subjects disobliged. Wherefore, as I have said, a new prince in his new government puts his subjects always into arms, as appears by several examples in history. But when a prince conquers a new State, and annexes it, as a member to his old, then it is necessary your subjects be disarmed, all but such as appeared for you in the conquest, and they are to be mollified by degrees, and brought into such a condition of laziness and effeminacy that in time your whole strength may devolve upon your own natural militia, which were trained up in your ancient dominion and are to be always about you. Our ancestors (and they were esteemed wise men) were wont to say that it was necessary to keep Pistoia by factions and Pisa by fortresses, and accordingly, in several towns under their subjection, they created and fomented factions and animosities, to keep them with more ease. This, at a time when Italy was unsettled and in a certain kind of suspense, might be well enough done, but I do not take it at this time for any precept for us, being clearly of opinion that the making of factions never does good, but that, where the enemy approaches and the city is divided, it must necessarily, and that suddenly, be lost, because the weaker party will always fall off to the enemy, and the other cannot be able to defend it. The Venetians (as I guess) upon the same grounds nourished the factions of the Guelfs and the Ghibilins in the cities under their jurisdiction; and though they kept them from blood, yet they encouraged their dissensions, to the end that the citizens, being employed among themselves, should have no time to conspire against them; which, as appeared afterwards, did not answer expectation, for being defeated at Valia, one of the said factions took arms and turned the Venetians out of their State. Such methods, therefore, as these do argue weakness in the prince; for no government of any strength or consistence will suffer such divisions, because they are useful only in time of peace, when perhaps they may contribute to the more easy management of their subjects, but when war comes the fallacy of those counsels is quickly discovered. Without doubt, princes grow great when they overcome the difficulties and impediments which are given them; and therefore Fortune, especially when she has a mind to exalt a new prince, who has greater need of reputation than a prince that is old and hereditary, raises him up enemies and encourages enterprises against him, that he may have opportunity to conquer them, and advance himself by such steps as his enemies had prepared. For which reason many have thought that a wise prince, when opportunity offers, ought, but with great cunning and address, to maintain some enmity against himself, that when time serves to destroy them, his own greatness may be increased.

Princes, and particularly those who are not of long standing, have found more fidelity and assistance from those whom they suspected at the beginning of their reign than from those who at first were their greatest confidants. Pandolfus Petrucci, Prince of Sienna, governed his State rather by those who were suspected than others. But this is not to be treated of largely, because it varies according to the subjects. I shall only say this, that those men who in the beginning of his government opposed him, if they be of such quality as to want the support of other people, are easily wrought over to the prince, and more strictly engaged to be faithful, because they knew that it must be their good carriage for the future that must cancel the prejudice that is against them; and so the prince comes to receive more benefit by them than by those who, serving him more securely, do most commonly neglect his affairs.

And seeing the matter requires, I will not omit to remind a prince who is but newly advanced, and that by some inward favour and correspondence in the country, that he considers well what it was that disposed those parties to befriend him; if it be not affection to him, but pique and animosity to the old government, it will cost much trouble and difficulty to keep them his friends, because it will be impossible to satisfy them; and upon serious disquisition, ancient and modern examples will give us the reason, and we shall find it more easy to gain such persons as were satisfied with the former government, and by consequence his enemies, than those who, being disobliged, sided with him and assisted to subvert it.

It has been a custom among princes, for the greater security of their territories, to build citadels and fortresses to bridle and restrain such as would enterprise against them, and to serve as a refuge in times of rebellion; and I approve the way because anciently practised, yet no longer ago than in our days, Nicolo Vitelli was known to dismantle two forts in the city of Castello, to secure his government; Guidobaldo, Duke of Urbin, returning to his State from whence Cæsar Borgia had driven him, demolished all the strong places in that province, and thereby thought it more unlikely again to fall into the hands of the enemy. The Bentivogli being returned to Bologna used the same course. So that fortresses are useful or not useful, according to the difference of time, and if in one place they do good, they do as much mischief in another. And the case may be argued thus: That prince who is more afraid of his subjects than neighbours, is to suffer them to stand; the family of the Sforzas has and will suffer more mischief by the Castle of Milan, which was built by Francesco Sforza, than by all its other troubles whatever; so that the best fortification of all is not to be hated by the people, for your fortresses will not protect you if the people have you in detestation, because they shall no sooner take arms but strangers will fall in and sustain them. In our times there is not one instance to be produced of advantage which that course has brought to any prince, but to the Countess of Furly, when, upon the death of Hieronimo, her husband, by means of those castles she was able to withstand the popular fury, and expect till supplies came to her from Milan and resettled her in the government; and as times then stood, the people were not in a condition to be relieved by any stranger. But afterwards they stood her in no stead when Cæsar Borgia invaded her, and the people, being incensed, joined with her enemy. Wherefore it had been better for her, both then and at first, to have possessed the affections of the people than all the castles in the country. These things being considered, I approve both of him that builds those fortresses and of him that neglects them, but must needs condemn him who relies so much upon them as to despise the displeasure of the people.

CHAPTER XXI

How a Prince is to demean himself to gain reputation.

Nothing recommends a prince so highly to the world as great enterprises and noble expressions of his own valour and conduct. We have in our days Ferdinand, King of Aragon—the present King of Spain—who may, and not improperly, be called a new prince, being of a small and weak king become for fame and renown the greatest monarch in Christendom; and if his exploits be considered you will find them all brave, but some of them extraordinary. In the beginning of his reign he invaded the kingdom of Granada, and that enterprise was the foundation of his grandeur. He began it leisurely, and without suspicion of impediment, holding the barons of Castile employed in that service, and so intent upon that war that they dreamt not of any innovation, whilst in the mean time, before they were aware, he got reputation and authority over them. He found out a way of maintaining his army at the expense of the Church and the people, and by the length of that war to establish such order and discipline among his soldiers, that afterwards they gained him many honourable victories. Besides this, to adapt him for greater enterprises (always making religion his pretence), by a kind of devout cruelty he destroyed and exterminated the Jews called Marrani, than which nothing could be more strange or deplorable. Under the same cloak of religion he invaded Africa, made his expedition into Italy, assaulted France, and began many great things which always kept the minds of his subjects in admiration and suspense, expecting what the event of his machinations would be. And these his enterprises had so sudden a spring and result one from the other that they gave no leisure to any man to be at quiet, or to continue anything against him. It is likewise of great advantage to a prince to give some rare example of his own administration at home (such is reported of Monsieur Bernardo da Milano), when there is occasion for somebody to perform anything extraordinary in the civil government, whether it be good or bad, and to find out such a way either to reward or punish him as may make him much talked of in the world. Above all, a prince is to have a care in all his actions to behave himself so as may give him the reputation of being excellent as well as great. A prince is likewise much esteemed when he shows himself a sincere friend or a generous enemy—that is, when without any hesitation he declares himself in favour of one against another, which, as it is more frank and princely, so it is more profitable than to stand neuter; for if two of your potent neighbours be at war, they are either of such condition that you are to be afraid of the victor or not; in either of which cases it will be always more for your benefit to discover yourself freely, and make a fair war. For in the first cause, if you do not declare, you shall be a prey to him who overcomes, and it will be a pleasure and satisfaction to him that is conquered to see you his fellow-sufferer; nor will anybody either defend or receive you, and the reason is, because the conqueror will never understand them to be his friends who would not assist him in his distress; and he that is worsted will not receive you because you neglected to run his fortune with your arms in your hands. Antiochus, upon the invitation of the Etolians, passed into Greece to repel the Romans. Antiochus sent ambassadors to the Achaians, who were in amity with the Romans, to persuade them to a neutrality, and the Romans sent to them to associate with them. The business coming to be debated in the Council of the Achaians, and Antiochus's ambassador pressing them to be neuters, the Roman ambassador replied: "As to what he has remonstrated, that it is most useful and most consistent with the interest of your State not to engage yourselves in our war, there is nothing more contrary and pernicious; for if you do not concern yourselves you will assuredly become a prey to the conqueror, without any thanks or reputation; and it will always be, that he who has the least kindness for you will tempt you to be neuters, but they that are your friends will invite you to take up arms." And those princes who are ill-advised, to avoid some present danger follow the neutral way, are most commonly ruined; but when a prince discovers himself courageously in favour of one party, if he with whom you join overcome, though he be very powerful, and you seem to remain at his discretion, yet he is obliged to you, and must needs have a respect for you, and men are not so wicked with such signal and exemplary ingratitude to oppress you. Besides, victories are never so clear and complete as to leave the conqueror without all sparks of reflection, and especially upon what is just. But if your confederate comes by the worst, you are received by him, and assisted whilst he is able, and becomest a companion of his fortune, which may possibly restore thee. In the second place, if they who contend be of such condition that they have no occasion to fear, let which will overcome, you are in prudence to declare yourself the sooner, because by assisting the one you contribute to the ruin of the other, whom, if your confederate had been wise, he ought rather to have preserved; so that he overcoming remains wholly at your discretion, and by your assistance he must of necessity overcome. And here it is to be noted, if he can avoid it, a prince is never to league himself with another more powerful than himself in an offensive war; because in that case if he overcomes you remain at his mercy, and princes ought to be as cautious as possible of falling under the discretion of other people. The Venetians, when there was no necessity for it, associated with France against the Duke of Milan, and that association was the cause of their ruin. But where it is not to be avoided, as happened to the Florentines when the Pope and the Spaniard sent their armies against Lombardy, there a prince is to adhere for the reasons aforesaid. Nor is any prince or government to imagine that in those cases any certain counsel can be taken, because the affairs of this world are so ordered that in avoiding one mischief we fall commonly into another. But a man's wisdom is most conspicuous where he is able to distinguish of dangers and make choice of the least; moreover, a prince to show himself a virtuoso, and honourer of all that is excellent in any art whatsoever. He is likewise to encourage and assure his subjects that they may live quietly in peace, and exercise themselves in their several vocations, whether merchandize, agriculture, or any other employment whatever, to the end that one may not forbear improving or embellishing his estate for fear it should be taken from him, nor another advancing his trade in apprehension of taxes; but the prince is rather to excite them by propositions of reward, and immunities to all such as shall any way amplify his territory or power. He is obliged, likewise, at convenient times in the year to entertain the people by feastings and plays, and spectacles of recreation; and, because all cities are divided into companies or wards, he ought to have respect to those societies, be merry with them sometimes, and give them some instance of his humanity and magnificence, but always retaining the majesty of his degree, which is never to be debased in any case whatever.

CHAPTER XXII

Of the Secretaries of Princes.

The election of his ministers is of no small importance to a prince, for the first judgment that is made of him or his parts is from the persons he has about him. When they are wise and faithful, be sure the prince is discreet himself, who, as he knew how to choose them able at first, so he has known how to oblige them to be faithful; but, when his ministers are otherwise, it reflects shrewdly upon the prince, for commonly the first error he commits is in the election of his servants. No man knew Antonia da Venafro to be secretary to Pandolfo Petrucci, Prince of Sienna, but he could judge Pandolfo to be a prudent man for choosing such a one as his minister. In the capacities and parts of men there are three sorts of degrees: one man understands of himself, another understands what is explained, and a third understands neither of himself nor by any explanation. The first is excellent, the second commendable, the third altogether unprofitable. If, therefore, Pandolfo was not in the first rank, he might be included in the second; for whenever a prince has the judgment to know the good and the bad of what is spoken or done, though his own invention be not excellent, he can distinguish a good servant from a bad, and exalt the one and correct the other; and the minister, despairing of deluding him, remains good in spite of his teeth.* But the business is, how a prince may understand his minister, and the rule for that is infallible.

---

* *Editor:* A strange use of this word, perhaps it indicates that when the servant disagrees with the prince, "he clenches his teeth" or "flatteringly lies through his teeth." The passage that follows shows how hard it is for a prince to learn the truth about himself. Another goes thus: "The servant cannot hope to deceive him, and is kept honest."

When you observe your officer more careful of himself than of you, and all his actions and designs pointing at his own interest and advantage, that man will never be a good minister, nor ought you ever to repose any confidence in him; for he who has the affairs of his prince in his hand ought to lay aside all thoughts of himself, and regard nothing but what is for the profit of his master. And, on the other side, to keep him faithful, the prince is as much concerned to do for him, by honouring him, enriching him, giving him good offices and preferments, that the wealth and honour conferred by his master may keep him from looking out for himself, and the plenty and goodness of his offices make him afraid of a change, knowing that without his prince's favour he can never subsist. When, therefore, the prince and the minister are qualified in this manner they may depend one upon the other; but when it is otherwise with them the end must be bad, and one of them will be undone.

CHAPTER XXIII

How Flatterers are to be avoided.

I will not pass by a thing of great consequence, being an error against which princes do hardly defend themselves, unless they be very wise and their judgment very good; and that is about flatterers, of which kind of cattle all histories are full; for men are generally so fond of their own actions, and so easily mistaken in them, that it is not without difficulty they defend themselves against those sort of people, and he that goes about to defend himself runs a great hazard of being despised; for there is no other remedy against flatterers than to let everybody understand you are not disobliged by telling the truth; yet if you suffer everybody to tell it you injure yourself and lessen your reverence. Wherefore a wise prince ought to go a third way, and select out of his State certain discreet men, to whom only he is to commit that liberty of speaking truth, and that of such things as he demands, and nothing else; but then he is to inquire of everything, hear their opinions, and resolve afterwards, as he pleases, and behave himself towards them in such sort that every one may find with how much the more freedom he speaks, with so much the more kindness he is accepted; that besides them he will hearken to nobody; that he considers well before he resolves; and that his resolutions, once taken, are never to be altered. He that does otherwise shall either precipitate his affairs by means of his flatterers, or by variety of advices often change his designs, which will lessen his esteem and render him contemptible. To this purpose I shall instance in one modern example.

Father Lucas, a servant to Maximilian, the present emperor, giving a character of his Majesty, declared him a person who never consulted anybody, and yet never acted according to his own judgment and inclination; and the reason was because he proceeded contrary to the prescriptions aforesaid—for the emperor is a close man, communicates his secrets to nobody, nor takes any man's advice; but when his determinations are to be executed and begin to be known in the world, those who are about him begin to discourage and dissuade him, and he, being good-natured, does presently desist. Hence it comes to pass that his resolutions of one day are dissolved in the next; no man knows what he desires or designs, nor no man can depend upon his resolutions. A prince, therefore, is always to consult, but at his own, not other people's pleasure, and rather to deter people from giving their advice undemanded; but he ought not to be sparing in his demands, nor when he has demanded, impatient of hearing the truth; but if he understands that any suppressed it and forbore to speak out for fear of displeasing, then, and not till then, he is to show his displeasure. And because there are those who believe that a prince which creates an opinion of his prudence in the people, does it not by any excellence in his own nature, but by the counsels of those who are about him, without doubt they are deceived; for this is a general and infallible rule—That that prince who has no wisdom of his own can never be well advised, unless by accident he commits all to the government and administration of some honest and discreet man. In this case it is possible things may be well ordered for awhile, but they can never continue, for his minister or vicegerent in a short time will set up for himself; but if a prince who has no great judgment of his own consults with more than one, their counsels will never agree, nor he have ever the cunning to unite them. Every man will advise according to his own interest or caprice, and he not have the parts either to correct or discover it; and other counsellors are not to be found, for men will always prove bad, unless by necessity they are compelled to be good. So then it is clear—That good counsels, from whomsoever they come, proceed rather from the wisdom of the prince than the prince's wisdom from the goodness of his counsels.

CHAPTER XXIV

*How it came to pass that the Princes of Italy
have most of them lost their dominions.*

The qualities aforesaid being observed, they make a new prince appear in the number of the more ancient, and render him presently more firm and secure in his government than if he had descended to it by right of inheritance; for the actions of a new prince are liable to stricter observation than if he were hereditary, and when they are known to be virtuous gain more upon people and oblige them further than antiquity of blood; because men are more affected with present than past things, and when in their present condition they find themselves well, they content themselves with it, without looking out anywhere else, employing themselves wholly in defence of their prince, unless in other things he be defective to himself; so that thereby he will have double honour in having laid the foundation of a new principality, and embellished and fortified it with good laws, good force, good friends, and good example; whereas he multiplies his disgrace, who, being born prince, loses his inheritance by his own ill-management and imprudence. And if the sovereign princes in Italy, who in our time have lost their dominions, be considered, as the King of Naples, the Duke of Milan, and others, there will be found in their beginning one common defect as to the management of their arms, for the reasons largely discoursed of before; besides, some of them will appear to have been hated by the people, or if they have had so much prudence as to preserve a friendship with them, they have been ignorant how to secure themselves against the grandees; for without these errors no States are lost that have money and strength enough to bring an army into the field. Philip of Macedon (not Alexander the Great's father, but he who was overcome by Titus Quintus) had no great force in comparison of the Romans and the Grecians which invaded him; yet, being a martial man, and one that understood how to insinuate with the people and oblige the nobility, he maintained war several years against both of them, and though at last he lost some towns, yet he kept his kingdom in spite of them. Those, therefore, of our princes who for many years together were settled in their principalities, if they lost them afterwards, they cannot accuse fortune, but their own negligence and indiscretion for not having in quiet times considered they might change (and it is the common infirmity of mankind in a calm to make no reckoning of a tempest) when adversity approached; they thought more of making their escape than defence, resting their whole hopes upon this, that when the people were weary of the insolence of the conqueror, they would recall them again; which resolution is tolerable indeed when others are wanting, but to neglect all other remedies and trust only to that, is much to be condemned, for a man would never throw himself down that another might take him up; besides, that may not happen, or if it does, not with your security, because that kind of defence is poor and depends not on yourself, and no defences are good, certain, and lasting, which proceed not from the prince's own courage and virtue.

CHAPTER XXV

How far in human affairs Fortune may avail,
and in what manner she may be resisted.

I am not ignorant that it is, and has been of old the opinion of many people, that the affairs of the world are so governed by fortune and Divine Providence that man cannot by his wisdom correct them, or apply any remedy at all; from whence they would infer that we are not to labour and sweat, but to leave everything to its own tendency and event. This opinion has obtained more in our days by the many and frequent revolutions which have been and are still seen beyond all human conjecture. And, when I think of it seriously sometimes, I am in some measure inclined to it myself; nevertheless, that our own free will may not utterly be exploded, I conceive it may be true that fortune may have the arbitrament of one-half of our actions, but that she leaves the other half, or little less, to be governed by ourselves. Fortune I do resemble to a rapid and impetuous river, which when swelled and enraged overwhelms the plains, subverts the trees and the houses, forces away the earth from one place and carries it to another; everybody fears, everybody shuns, but nobody knows how to resist it; yet though it be thus furious sometimes, it does not follow but when it is quiet and calm men may by banks and fences, and other provisions, correct it in such manner that when it swells again it may be carried off by some canal, or the violence thereof rendered less licentious and destructive. So it is with fortune, which shows her power where there is no predisposed virtue to resist it, and turns all her force and impetuosity where she knows there are no banks, no fences to restrain her. If you consider Italy (the seat of all these revolutions), and what it was that caused them, you will find it an open field, without any bounds or ramparts to secure it; and that, had it been defended by the courage of their ancestors, as Germany and Spain and France have been, those inundations had never happened, or never made such devastation as they have done. And this I hold sufficient to have spoken in general against fortune. But restraining myself a little more to particulars, I say it is ordinary to see a prince happy one day and ruined the next, without discerning any difference in his humour or government; and this I impute to the reasons of which I have discoursed largely before; and one of them is, because that prince which relies wholly upon fortune, being subject to her variations, must of necessity be ruined. I believe, again, that prince may be happy whose manner of proceeding concerts with the times, and he unhappy who cannot accommodate to them; for in things leading to the end of their designs (which every man has in his eye, and they are riches and honour), we see men have various methods of proceeding. Some with circumspection, others with heat; some with violence, others with cunning; some with patience, and others with fury; and every one, notwithstanding the diversity of their ways, may possibly attain them. Again, we see two persons equally cautious, one of them prospers, and the other miscarries; and on the other side, two equally happy by different measures, one being deliberate, and the other as hasty; and this proceeds from nothing but the condition of the times, which suits or does not suit with the manner of their proceedings. From hence arises what I have said, that two persons by different operations do attain the same end, whilst two others steer the same course, and one of them succeeds and the other is ruined. From hence, likewise, may be reduced the vicissitudes of good; for if to one who manages with deliberation and patience, the times and conjuncture of affairs come about so favourably that his conduct be in fashion, he must needs be happy; but if the face of affairs and the times change, and he changes not with them, he is certainly ruined. Nor is there any man to be found so wise that knows how to accommodate or frame himself to all these varieties, both because he cannot deviate from that to which Nature has inclined him; as likewise because, if a man has constantly prospered in one way, it is no easy matter to persuade him to another; and he that is so cautious, being at a loss when time requires he should be vigorous, must of necessity be destroyed; whereas, if he could turn with the times, his fortune would never betray him. Pope Julius XI. in all his enterprises acted with passion and vehemence, and the times and accident of affairs were so suitable to his manner of proceeding that he prospered in whatever he undertook. Consider his expedition of Bolonia in the days of Monsieur

Giovanni Bentivogli; the Venetians were against it, and the Kings of Spain and France were in treaty, and had a mind to it themselves; yet he with his promptitude and fury undertook it personally himself, and that activity of his kept both Spaniard and Venetian in suspense (the Venetians for fear, the Spaniards in hopes to recover the whole kingdom of Naples), and the King of France came over to his side; for seeing him in motion, and desirous to make him his friend, and thereby to correct the insolence of the Venetian, he thought he could not deny him his assistance without manifest injustice; so that Julius with his rashness and huffing★ did that which never any other Pope could have done with all his cunning and insinuation, for had he deferred his departure from Rome till all things had been put into exact order, and his whole progress concluded, as any other Pope would have done, he could never have succeeded; the king of France would have pretended a thousand excuses, and others would have suggested twice as many fears. I will pass by the rest of his enterprises, which were all alike and prospered as well, and the shortness of his life secured him against change; for had the times fallen out so that he had been forced to proceed with accurate circumspection, he would have certainly been ruined, for he could never have left those ways to which his nature inclined him. I conclude, then, that whilst the obstinacy of princes consists with the motion of fortune, it is possible they may be happy; but when once they disagree, the poor prince comes certainly to the ground. I am of opinion, likewise, that it is better to be hot and precipitate than cautious and apprehensive; for fortune is a woman, and must be hectored to keep her under; and it is visible every day she suffers herself to be managed by those who are brisk and audacious rather than by those who are

---

★ *Editor:* A bluff.

cold and phlegmatic in their motions,* and therefore, like a woman, she is always a friend to those who are young, because being less circumspect they attack her with more security and boldness.†

CHAPTER XXVI

An Exhortation to deliver Italy from the Barbarians.

Having weighed, therefore, all that is said before, and considered seriously with myself whether in this juncture of affairs in Italy the times were disposed for the advancement of a new prince, and whether there was competent matter that could give occasion to a virtuous and wise person to introduce such a form as would bring reputation to him and benefit to all his subjects, it seems to me that at this present so many things concur to the exaltation of a new prince that I do not know any time that has been more proper than this; and if, as I said before, for the manifestation of the courage of Moses it was necessary that the Israelites should be captives in Egypt; for discovery of the magnanimity of Cyrus, that the Persians should be oppressed by the Medes; and for the illustration of the excellence of Theseus that the Athenians should be banished and dispersed; so to evince and demonstrate the courage of an Italian spirit it was necessary that Italy should be reduced to its present condition; that it should be in greater bondage than the Jews, in greater servitude than the Persians, and in greater dispersion than the Athenians; without

---

* *Editor:* Emotions.
† *Editor: The Prince* is remarkably modern in its approach to human nature; only in this paragraph does Machiavelli reflect the attitude of his age. But even so, there are grains of truth in his words.

head, without order, harassed, spoiled, overcome, overrun, and overflown with all kind of calamity; and though formerly some sparks of virtue have appeared in some persons that might give it hopes that God had ordained them for its redemption, yet it was found afterwards that in the very height and career of their exploits they were checked and forsaken by fortune, and poor Italy left half dead, expecting who would be her Samaritan to bind up her wounds, put an end to the sackings and devastations in Lombardy, the taxes and expilations in the kingdom of Naples and Tuscany, and cure her sores which length of time had festered and imposthumated. It is manifest how she prays to God daily to send some person who may redeem her from the cruelty and insolence of the barbarians. It is manifest how prone and ready she is to follow the banner that any man will take up; nor is it at present to be discerned where she can repose her hopes with more probability than in your illustrious family, which by its own courage and interest and the favour of God and the Church (of which it is now chief), may be induced to make itself head in her redemption; which will be no hard matter to be effected if you lay before you the lives and actions of the persons above-named; who though they were rare and wonderful were yet but men, and not accommodated with so fair circumstances as you. Their enterprise was not more just nor easy, nor God Almighty more their friend than yours. You have justice on your side; for that war is just which is necessary,★ and it is piety to fight where no hope is left in anything else. The people are universally disposed, and where the disposition is so great the opposition can be but small, especially you taking your rules from those persons which I have proposed to you for a model. Besides, many things that they did were supernatural, and by

---

★ *Editor:* A "just war" was a popular medieval concept.

God's immediate conduct the sea opened, a cloud directed, a rock afforded water, it rained manna, all these things are recompensed in your grandeur, and the rest remains to be executed by you. God will not do everything immediately, because He will not deprive us of our free will and the honour that devolves upon us. Nor is it any wonder if none of the aforenamed Italians have been able to do that which may be hoped for from your illustrious family;* and if in so many revolutions in Italy, and so long continuation of war, their military virtue seems spent and extinguished, the reason is, their old discipline was not good, and nobody was able to direct a better. Nothing makes so much to the honour of a new prince as new laws and new orders invented by him, which, if they be well founded, and carry anything of grandeur along with them, do render him venerable and wonderful; and Italy is susceptible enough of any new form. Their courage is great enough in the soldier if it be not wanting in the officer; witness the duels and combats, in which the Italians have generally the better by their force and dexterity and stratagem; but come to their battles, and they have oftener the worst, and all from the inexperience of their commanders; for those who pretend to have skill will never obey, and every one thinks he has skill,† there having been nobody to this very day raised by his virtue and fortune to that height of reputation as to prevail with others to obey him. Hence it came that, in so long time, in the many wars during the last twenty years, whenever an army consisted wholly of Italians it was certainly beaten; and this may be testified by Tarus, Alexandria, Capua, Genoa, Vaila, Bologna, and Mestri. If, therefore, your illustrious family be in-

---

* *Editor:* Machiavelli addresses this chapter specifically to Lorenzo de' Medici. Other chapters could apply to other princes, but not this one.
† *Editor:* A point not to be underestimated, "The clown will always wish to play Hamlet."

clined to follow the examples of those excellent persons who redeemed their countries, it is necessary, as a true fundamental of all great enterprises, to provide yourselves with forces of your own subjects, for you cannot have more faithful nor better soldiers than they. And though all of them be good, yet altogether they will be much better when they find themselves not only commanded but preferred and caressed by a prince of their own. It is necessary, therefore, to be furnished with these forces before you can be able with Italian virtue to vindicate your country from the oppression of strangers. And though the Swiss and Spanish infantry be counted terrible, they have both of them their defects; and a third sort may be composed that may not only encounter but be confident to beat them; for the Spanish foot cannot deal with horse, and the Swiss are not invincible when they meet with foot as obstinate as themselves. It has been seen by experience, and would be so again, the Spaniards cannot sustain the fury of the French cavalry, and the Swiss have been overthrown by the infantry of Spain. And though of this last we have seen no perfect experiment, yet we had a competent essay at the battle of Ravenna, where the Spanish foot being engaged with the German battalions (which observe the same order and discipline with the Swiss), the Spaniards, by the agility of their bodies and the protection of their bucklers, broke in under their pikes and killed them securely, while the poor Germans were incapable to defend themselves; and had not the Spaniards been charged by the horse, the German foot had been certainly cut off. It is possible, therefore, the defect of both those foot being known, to institute a third which may buckle with the horse and be in no fear of their foot; which will be effected not by the variation of their arms but by changing their discipline. And these are some of those things which, being newly reformed, give great grandeur and reputation to any new prince. This opportunity, therefore, is by no means to be slipped, that Italy, after so long expectation, may see some hopes of deliverance. Nor can it be expressed with what joy, with what impatience of revenge, with what fidelity, with what compassion, with what tears such a champion would be received into all the provinces that have suffered by those barbarous inundations. What gates would be shut against him? What people would deny him obedience? What malice would oppose him? What true Italian would refuse to follow him? There is not, there is not anybody but abhors and nauseates this barbarous domination. Let your illustrious family, then, address itself to the work with as much courage and confidence as just enterprises are undertaken; that under their ensigns our country may be recovered, and under their conduct Petrarch's prophecy may be fulfilled, who has promised that—

> *Virtu contr' al furore*
> *Prendera l'arme, and fia il combatter Corto.*
> *Che l'antico valore*
> *Ne' gl' Italici curr' non e ancor morto.*

Virtue shall arm 'gainst rage, and in short fight
Prove the *Roman* valour's not extinguish'd quite.

The Servant

ALISTAIR MCALPINE

To the most magnificent, Baroness Thatcher of Kesteven,
Prime Minister of Great Britain 1979–1990,
from one of her many servants,
who believes she could have been better served.

When he wrote *The Prince,* Machiavelli was presenting himself for a job. Of all the activities of idle men, politics can be the most exciting, and those like Machiavelli left stranded by its tides will always try to return. Machiavelli believed that through his knowledge of history he could show a Prince how to conduct himself, how to apply techniques learned from historical events to his advantage. But history is a fallible guide, and it is curious that a man seeking employment from a successful Prince should presume to advise him on his conduct. Instead of instructing the Prince, a more Machiavellian Machiavelli would have written a book advising the Servants of Princes. The Prince, identifying a talent for service, would have hired him on the spot, granting Machiavelli the influence he so desired. That book, which might also have been called *The Servant,* would have explained not how Machiavelli could assist the Prince in governing his country, but how he would serve him by dealing on his behalf as the Prince acted in matters great and small: clearing a path for the Prince to rule, managing day by day those around him. Such a book would recognize that while politicians have the same frailties and failings, fears and conceits as all other human beings, they live in a closeted environment which heightens their senses and makes them act irrationally. It is because politicians are human yet may not behave like other humans that the Servant cannot be totally straightforward. On occasions the Servant needs to deceive and mislead—not for pleasure or gain, but to ensure the success of the Idea and the Prince. This book tries to show some of the devices that can be used to ensure the advancement of the Idea through securing the rule of the Prince.

The Idea is unique to the Prince. The Idea is the philosophy on which the Prince will base all of his actions. The Idea incorporates the Prince's aims and ambitions for his people. The Idea explains how the Prince's kingdom will grow and how it will compete with the kingdoms of other leaders. The Idea will become the touchstone for the morals of his people. The Idea starts with the Prince, and while men and women may say that they advise the Prince, they will really be attracted by the power of the Idea. It is from the Idea that the Prince draws his strength. The Prince needs the Idea in order to be able to take the necessary decisions to gain power in the land and then hold on to that power. Without the Idea this man is nothing.

In this book when I speak of the Prince I do not mean just any leader. I speak of the perfect Prince, with all the nobility of spirit that the greatest of Princes should have. The Prince governs for the benefit of the people. The Prince governs only for this reason. It is to promote the Idea that the Prince rules. He is not a Prince who merely by chance finds himself in charge of the affairs of other men. If the Prince finds that after a time other men have frustrated his intention of carrying out his Idea and so decides to change his Idea, then he must cease to be the Prince. In just holding a job his conduct is such that he is not truly the Prince, not a leader for the Servant to serve and not a man to be trusted with the Idea. It has been said that there is nothing so powerful as an idea when its time is come. The Servant's role is to serve the Prince in the implementation of the Idea, to do what he can to ensure the time *is* the right one.

The Servant is the instrument of the Prince and the Idea, not of the state. The state has its own servants, who owe it their loyalty, because Princes and Ideas inevitably change.

In these pages, when I speak of the Servant I mean perhaps one man, or possibly the leader's private office. I do not speak of the whole of the Prince's court, or the cabinet of a political leader, although the collective Servant can contain members of a court or a cabinet. I will in this work speak of the concept of service on its highest possible plane. The difference between the Prince and the Servant is that the Prince as a ruler has power: the Servant could use power, power that comes from his relationship with the Prince, but chooses to use influence instead. It is the Servant's job to help explain the Idea to its followers, to enlist and to organize their support. The Servant will use the Idea to inspire the wealthy supporters of the Prince and collect from them large sums. The Servant will also use the Idea to raise small sums from the multitude of people, for if a man supports an idea with his money, no matter how small the sum, then that support can generally be relied upon at moments when the Prince's right to rule is tested. This money that the Servant raises will be used to run the Prince's campaign, to purchase the advice of experts in the arts of influencing the opinion of the people. The Prince's essential task is to formulate and preach the Idea, but although the Servant will organize his campaigns, it is vital that the direction of these campaigns lies exclusively in the hands of the Prince. It is of the utmost importance that the Prince knows that it is he who won the throne, and he alone. Afterwards many will claim the glory for these victories, of course. But the Prince who was indeed placed in power by other men's efforts appreciates that he can also be removed by their efforts, will live always with this thought and will rule with uncertainty. The Prince who wins by his own efforts will feel secure, although when men tell of the battles fought to win that power he will not wish to hear others take any credit that he himself has not bestowed.

People will find it hard to trust a Prince who comes to power through fortune or who is implicated with those who have stolen power. He must always beware, for in moments when he is weak the people will remember this of him. A Prince can rule only with an Idea—can only rule with lasting success, that is—and having stolen power without an Idea he can merely play the part of a Prince, waiting for others to pull him down.* The Servant must orchestrate the Prince's campaigns, for he understands the working of organizations. The Prince may by chance understand organizations, but he must concentrate on directing the thrust of his campaigns and preaching the Idea. Ideas need an organization to make their time come, but an organization is completely different from an Idea. An Idea increases in strength by staying the same, while an organization increases in strength by changing opportunistically. Experience is of great advantage to an organization, of no advantage to an Idea. Only if the Idea is not adulterated will it come to dominance.

The Servant will understand the grandeur of his role, for in the heart of every Servant there lies a Prince—a desire to be noble and brave and successful. It is proper that this should be so, for the Prince is a symbol of all these things. But, Servant, let that inner Prince lie still, for ambition is easily spotted and becomes the wasting disease of the able Servant. Contain this

---

Editor: This was particularly true of the British Prime Minister John Major, the conservative successor to Margaret Thatcher, who was believed by an influential few to have stolen the office.

force, this ambition, and use its energy only in the service of your master, and in time you may become a Prince among Servants.

To carry out his work the Servant will need a myth—by which I mean the sum of a variety of personae which the Servant assumes. The myth is how the Servant disguises himself while moving among his contemporaries, it is the facade behind which the Servant hides from those who would know him well. This is not the careful rearrangement of his character for the benefit of future historians, but a device that the Servant uses in his daily contact with people who see him often and know him well. Indispensable to the Servant, the myth must be chosen with care, but not because this is how the Servant would like to appear to his fellow men—the true Servant would never engage in such conceit. The Servant's myth is chosen solely for its ability to help the Servant to serve the Idea and the Prince. The myth of the Servant has three main strands: love, fear and hate. Loyalty plays no part in the world inhabited by Princes and their Servants, and to believe in it leads only to betrayal and deep disappointment. Loyalty is the stuff of romantic novelists, the attribute of faithful dogs and horses. In the circle of the Prince and the Servant loyalties change with circumstances. If by chance you find loyalty, be grateful, but never expect loyalty or assume it in your plans. Is the Servant loyal? He is loyal to the Prince and the Idea, but only to both because he believes in both, and only while both are joined together. Belief is a much stronger instinct than loyalty: loyalty is the emotion which remains after belief has died.

Machiavelli says that the Prince should endeavour 'to escape being hated', but hatred forms a strand in the Servant's myth. Although it must be perfumed and powdered and heavily disguised, a little hatred in a myth hones it like a sharpening stone. It gives the myth force, but, most importantly, it is the flaw which will give it credibility. Fear is another ingredient. It is always useful to be a little feared, though the fear must be inspired by the position held rather than by the man himself.

On the other hand, love should be present in abundance, since it helps disguise the less attractive aspects of strength. Love suggests commitment, a very attractive quality; it also suggests that there is a weakness in the Servant—that he is capable of irrational thought, that for those he loves there is no point beyond which he will not go. Remember that I am talking of the Servant's myth, not the Servant in truth. While the Servant may or may not be capable of love, he allows no true love to touch his judgement. Love is a very important factor, for if the Servant will convince others of the Idea, he must first fall in love with it himself. Love is the most powerful weapon of a Servant who would change people's minds, for some, seeing how much the Servant loves the Idea, will pay attention to it, and others, seeing how the Servant loves them, will listen to him. If the Servant is to convince a man of an Idea, he must love the man. If the man is objectionable, the Servant must never say so; indeed, he must never even think that this man is objectionable—thoughts communicate quite as easily as words. Love for another is the highest form of flattery because it seems to the beloved an endorsement of their views, which is vital if you would change those views. When I use the word 'love' I use it in an emotional sense; the Servant must never be drawn into physical contact with someone whose mind he seeks to change. Lesser men than the Servant may lust after the body of another, and may excuse this lust to themselves saying, 'I love this one and seduce this one in the interests of my occupation, for it will help my career, and in the interests of the Prince, for by this physical love I can change this one's mind.' This is a trap, a self delusion; have none of it.

There are, of course, many other strands in the Servant's myth besides love, fear and hate, but these three provide the essential emotional foundation for his work. This myth must be believed by all but the Servant himself. He must, before he engages in myth-making, discover the nature of his true character. Only then will he be able in times of great difficulty to tell the difference between himself and his myth, between the truth and the perceived truth. The Servant moves like a shadow behind his own myth. Yet although he may cynically construct the myth, which he knows to be a device, the Idea he must truly believe in; he must allow no cynicism to creep into the Idea. As he exploits his myth, directing it to take this or that action, he must take care not to destroy it. It must be so constructed that, when he is carrying out his tasks, the Servant does not find himself in conflict with the myth. There will be occasions when events are so dire that the Servant has to take action that brings him into conflict with the myth. When creating the myth it is well to take this into account. Reasons for such conflict must be built into the myth and carefully concealed, only to be revealed in an emergency. Revealing them will explain to the population this apparent inconsistency in the Servant's character. Although the myth and the actions of the Servant are sometimes totally different, and indeed can operate in different directions at the same time, the Servant must never have to choose between necessary action and his myth. This will give the Servant great strength, for people will judge him by what they know of his myth. People like to be reassured; the public respect uniform, both military and civilian, and like to believe that they know exactly what they are dealing with. The people, never truly knowing the Servant, will never truly know how he will behave.

If it becomes publicly known that the Servant and his myth are not one and the same thing, then the Servant would do well to consider early retirement and a career in agriculture. Agriculture, or gardening which is its most civilized form, is a wonderful occupation for retired politicians. The most famous garden in Su Chou was created by a Chinese Chancellor of the Exchequer, who built the Humble Administrator's garden while temporarily retired from politics. The Servant must recognize that to deceive others is often admirable but to deceive oneself is detestable: the myth and the Servant are secondary to the Idea. He must always remember this.

The Prince, the Idea and the Servant are the three legs of a stool; without any one of them, the stool will topple; each one is as important as the other, and each has its own distinct function. In *The Prince,* Machiavelli catches something of this when he directs that 'Princes should delegate to others the enactment of unpopular measures and keep in their own hands the distribution of favours.' This is the only sign in *The Prince* of a shared relationship between the Servant and the Prince. Over the centuries, Machiavelli has acquired a reputation for political cunning: in the popular mind 'Machiavellian behaviour' is associated with dirt, dishonesty and double-dealing. Although I recommend all of these in some form and more besides, I believe there is an essential nobility about the concept of the Prince, the Idea and the Servant working in unison. However dubious the means may look, this trinity fosters good government, and it is only when these three forces work together that nations can be governed with success. I do not claim that the failure of any one of these forces will destroy a nation, but I do claim that the effect of the three united, being a noble concept, will bring nobility to the state.

The whole object of this book is to show some of the devices that the Servant may deploy to help keep the Prince in power so he may carry out the Idea. The Servant's task is to see that nobody hinders the implementation of the Idea. This is not a handbook for those who would compromise. Quite the reverse: it would cast out trimmers of all sorts. Here you will find no easy advice or half measures, and acting on the information here will demand sacrifice. But the outcome can be triumph.

These notes on the conduct of the Servant are collected from many sources. For example, the relationship between the Prince and the Servant is not unlike the relationship between Mr Pickwick and Mr Sam Weller, a man who glorified in the concept of service, or between Bertie Wooster and Jeeves. Dickens and Wodehouse are not authors aspiring politicians normally go to for advice; but they could do worse.

The exercise of power is evident when everybody knows who has achieved a certain objective. The exercise of influence is when the same thing happens and nobody knows who has instigated it. Power is the declining state of a man who previously had influence. The Servant is a man of influence. If the Servant ever gives way to the temptation to exercise power, he can no longer serve and should be dismissed, for in the desire to exercise power, the Servant reveals an ambition to be the Prince. The Servant thereby also reveals his folly and his conceit, for he should know that it is much more satisfying to be influential than to be powerful. There is only one form of power that the Servant may, from time to time, indulge in: the power to thwart the ambitions of others, or negative power. This is the most fun of all.

Whatever people's motives may appear to be, it is their real desires that matter. The Servant should not attempt to attribute motives to men's actions, for these are irrelevant. It is only actions that count. What future generations think of the motives of the Prince is likewise immaterial. The Servant lives for today, and he must use this fact to the advantage of the Prince.

The Servant has no interest in the future, nor must he allow thoughts of how history will judge the Prince to influence his actions. He must also shape the past to suit the Prince. Memories of other ages are recorded by historians who have scant regard for the evidence. These historians who try to please one group or another always distort the facts, which are further changed by fashion and politics over the years. This 'history' is then produced by men, like Machiavelli, as useful evidence for making decisions. The contemporary record of newspapers likewise becomes fact for historians, but, just as Hitler and Stalin rewrote history, so newspapers rewrite the present. The Prince, the Servant and their followers might just as well throw a handful of corn in the air and make decisions based on the shapes these seeds make when they fall to the ground. At least this will tell you which way the wind is blowing, and with what force. When making decisions, the Servant must reject history and the work of historians. History is useful only to the extent that it can justify actions the Prince has already decided upon.

In certain matters of fact—births, deaths, the outcome of battles—it would seem impossible to reinterpret history. For instance, it could not be argued that Napoleon won the Battle of Waterloo. However, it could be argued that it was either Blücher or Wellington who did win that battle. Even in great events there is scope for a particular interpretation. In smaller events the truth is often so obscure that even the people involved seldom know the actual truth, only the truth as they see it. Hence this becomes the perceived truth, and although it could be wrong, for all intents and purposes it is the truth. Most people believe the truth to be constant; in fact truth is what people believe. The Servant, knowing this, can create his own truths.

It is important to understand that an accepted fact is more powerful than the truth. Take miracles: the real truth is known only to God. The people who saw a miracle believe it; many people who did not see it do not believe it. The Servant is not a seeker after absolute truth, but one who will take the view that best suits the Prince. The Servant will then promote that view until it becomes an established fact. As the argument moves away from the truth to the perceived truth, so the Servant has the evidence of his newly made 'facts' to base his argument on. Even though it may be far from the truth, the fact, once established, will be generally agreed on by all. Thus it will seem a true fact as opposed to a false fact, or a lie. Let not the Servant base his argument on the laziness of a lie when true facts can be so easily summoned by his own skill.

Take the miracle of Fatima, which took place in Portugal in 1936. People saw, or believed that they saw, the sun spin towards the earth. Others believed that the laws of science cannot be suspended, and so disbelieved the miracle. Whether the miracle did in fact occur or not is of no consequence—it is how men believe that matters. Why disbelieve the eyewitness accounts of some, but believe those others who say that such an event is impossible? The truth is beyond the capacity of men to prove one way or the other. A miracle, like any event, will be believed and understood according to the way it is promoted.

Some men may challenge the assertions of the Servant, but when they do so they challenge what people generally believe. Unless they are engaged in folly they will not do this. This is why the Servant will not challenge the general views of the people, but rather use their views to base his arguments on. Old concepts can be powerful, and can provide a good base for the Idea, though they will never produce the Idea.

Machiavelli writes of a number of rulers who chose to murder their Servants once they had achieved power. Of course, it is very hard to employ anybody at all competent if you have a reputation for murdering them, and this is the stuff of fifteenth- and sixteenth-century Italy, but it does indicate that the Servant must consider very carefully the Prince whom he has helped to power. Consequently, the Servant must behave as if the time before his leader became the Prince does not exist. Sometimes Princes like to boast of their achievements to show just how far they have risen. When they do so, the Servant must never suggest that he helped in any way. Instead, the Servant might indicate to the newly established Prince that he was always a Prince in spirit, and that it was only a question of time before he became a Prince in name.

The Prince will know how to deal with established institutions. These are powerful forces; the Servant must realize this and treat their representatives with caution and courtesy, for in dangerous and complicated matters, there is no substitute for courtesy. This moves all kinds of people; never can there be too much courtesy in a Servant.

Recruits to the Idea must be made all the time. Sometimes the Servant will have to use his myth to make the Idea acceptable to those who resist it; the Servant will, with the help of the myth, obscure the Idea, but never will he attempt to change it. The Idea will always be clear to its true followers, but the support of fellow travellers is necessary, and if they do not fully understand what it is they are supporting, the Servant will just have to come to terms with that.

Machiavelli proposed simply to destroy all opposition after taking power, but that option does not work any longer amongst civilized peoples. It may yet apply to a few particularly selfish individuals, who can be destroyed by cunning rather than force, but it ought never to be tried on ideas. An idea is like certain plants; the more it is cut down, the stronger it becomes.

Nevertheless, the Servant must not allow himself to be put into a position where he appears to ally himself with any idea except the Prince's, for the Prince will feel jealous of other ideas and thus, by association, of the Servant himself. These other ideas fall into two categories: the active and the passive. For instance, religion is a passive idea: religion can coexist with other ideas; religion is not exclusive. It is important that while he does not himself become involved in it, the Servant treats religion with respect. (I include within religion ideas like the masonic movement, clubs and other men's associations.) It is vital that the Servant is not involved in situations where his emotional loyalty to the Prince may be tested, or where people think that by recruiting the Prince's Servant they have earned an advantage with the Prince. Treat all these organizations with courtesy; nothing more.

Other ideas, such as communism, socialism, conservatism, fascism and many more, are in this context active ideas: they are, or seek to be, exclusive of each other, and will be opposed by the Prince. He has his own Idea. The Servant must encourage and assist in the opposition of these ideas, for to oppose them with the Prince's own Idea, if done with vigour, can only make the Prince's Idea more vigorous. The Servant must attack these other ideas, although he must always show kindness and courtesy to their protagonists. This will be quite unexpected and will not be returned, thus ensuring that the Servant has the goodwill of disinterested observers. The Servant must be sure that he fully understands these opposing ideas. The Servant always learns before he acts and never attacks blindly.

Perhaps because he was an historian, Machiavelli advises the Prince to follow in the path of history, but history repeats itself only through an absence of originality in mankind. The Prince is unique and must be encouraged to think out problems afresh. After all, the Prince's enemies can read books as well. Originality should also be reflected in the way that the Servant carries out the Prince's plans. It is the Prince's Idea which will succeed or fail. If the Idea is strong enough, it can spread like morning mist. Without the Idea, no man can be the Prince. There will be times when the Idea is uncomfortable; then the Servant and his myth will have to play their full part.

The Prince, at times, may find that he has a great desire to be an ordinary man. However, Princes are not ordinary men, and under no circumstances must they be allowed to think that they are. It is the job of the Servant to reassure the Prince of that, constantly reminding him of his position. It may be that this desire of the Prince to be an ordinary man is brought about by an inclination to indulge in some of the vices of the ordinary man. This is unlikely in one who is truly the Prince; it is entirely possible, however, in one who would be the Prince, and in those who are born Princes it is almost certain, for they have an arrogance unique to their breeding. As far as he can, the Servant must observe and keep silent, hiding his knowledge even from the Prince. But he dare not let anyone else have access to this side of the Prince. The character of the people introduced to the Prince must never interfere with the running of the state. A Servant who arranges these things lives with fear. If the Servant has to become involved, then he must have well prepared his myth, for he will surely need it; nothing must be allowed to jeopardize the Idea.

There is a device that the Servant may find useful from time to time; that device is called the 'false accusation'. The Servant encourages his enemies to accuse him of some discreditable action or other, preferably the sort of action that the Servant clearly has no desire to commit. The Servant then allows all and

sundry to believe that he is guilty. At the moment when the enemies of the Servant are celebrating the great currency achieved
by their accusation, forgetting all other things of which they
might accuse the Servant, it is proved by physical circumstances
that the Servant could not possibly be guilty. The enemies of the
Servant are discredited and it is hard, even impossible for them
to accuse him of other misdeeds. This device of the mistaken
accusation has been the salvation of more than one guilty man.★

The Prince will have around him ministers who are both capable and cunning. All these men are rivals of the Prince and,
since they know the Servant to have the ear of the Prince and wish
to remain on friendly terms, will only tell him what they want the
Prince to hear. These men cannot all be destroyed, but one of
them should be posted to some unruly province or place with an
uncertain future, as an example on which the others can reflect.

These rivals will try to persuade the Prince to move away
from his Idea so that they can destroy the Prince and succeed
him. The Prince must not be driven from his Idea or he will fall,
and as he falls, so will the Servant. The Servant's job is to hinder,
both in secret and in public, through the use of strategies and
technicalities, any attempt to change the Idea. The whole reason
for his service lies in the preservation of the Idea and the Prince.

The problem facing the Prince is how to promote his Idea,
control his colleagues and at the same time make the population happy. The Idea, if it remains pure, will be too strong for

---

★ *Editor:* This passage refers to the Geoffrey Archer libel action. A writer of popular books, politician, and lately a leading candidate as Mayor of London, Archer
has been forced to withdraw as new evidence has been produced that may affect
the results of that libel action. A popular newspaper had apparently wrongly accused him of sleeping with a prostitute. While this action made his dubious reputation fireproof, after this, whatever the newspapers wrote of him, had no affect
on his political life, he went on to become a member of the House of Lords.

potential dissenters, for colleagues will not desert an Idea that is operating successfully for one that is not. They may aspire to be Princes, but they are mere soldiers. They will desert when they think that the Idea has become so devalued as to become indistinguishable from others. The people may then wonder if, in practice, the Idea is really to their benefit and grow to dislike it. In this case their emotions must be tapped by the Prince, who in his preaching of the Idea must reject any suggestion of doubt.

The Servant must cultivate his myth. He does this by appearing in a variety of personalities to a variety of carefully chosen people, then making certain that, at the right time, all these people meet. The result is confusion and, as people prefer order, they will invent a larger, more complex personality for him—based on the evidence that the Servant has given to each of them. This personality the Servant may then adjust before spreading it, and developing his myth. Without it, he will be just another official of the court. It goes without saying that the Servant must be a man of competence, but however competent he may be, all will be lost without the myth. It need have no connection with reality; the Servant can be naturally cruel or kind; it will make no difference provided he attends to his myth. The myth of the Servant must never be confused with the Idea of the Prince, which is his alone.

The Servant deals in controlled confusion. He allows people to believe their own inventions about his life and background by using people who are in the habit of gossiping. He will let carefully placed disinformation build up a picture in their minds. When some say evil he will find others who will say only good of him, and out of this contradiction the Servant will take those parts that he needs in the construction of his myth, and have them repeated by men of authority in matters of gossip. So one man will say to another, 'I know this man; he is clearly this or that. I can tell you this in confidence.' And the man to whom he says these things will say, 'You make a great mistake when you say this about the Servant. I happen to know the truth.' And this one will repeat what he has been told, because men can always be relied upon to repeat matters that they are told in confidence. Soon these things about the Servant will be written down and will become the perceived truth—which is known to be very far from the truth.

Most of his battles will be fought quietly, for that is how the Servant prefers to influence actions: by changing the order in which events happen, for example, so that opponents discover that what they oppose has altered, though they find it hard to identify how. In open warfare, however, the myth of the Servant requires a degree of aggression, possibly a little crudity. This is what people expect in warfare, and the myth of the Servant should always be predictable. In peacetime, the myth depends on his kindness and sympathy, for this is the nature of peace, and thus, predictable. While the appearance of predictability is important, this should not imply that the Servant himself cannot be flexible in practice. It is the Servant's myth that is predictable.

The Servant must have assistants who will stay with him long enough to know how he works, but not too long. A good employee will probably take five years to rise, and then have five years at his best, followed by five years of decline when his energy is beginning to fail. All those who would hold a high position should remember that it is in the last years that they will be most loved, since people tend to love and respect those who, having been many years in the same post, do not have much longer to serve. The Servant knows this—and he knows that it is the prospect of their going that the people love.

The Servant must give credit for his rise as often as he can to others, and attribute any successes he may have to these men. Often they will be men of little account, so the Servant will construct legends about them to advance their prestige.

The Servant must be a good judge of men and how they will behave. This is a difficult art, as we are all inclined to see other men in the light that suits us. The Servant does not need to judge men's talents so much as to spot the changes in them. Even a physical alteration in a man—a loss of weight, a new style of dress—may indicate a change in his actions, and can serve as a warning to the Servant. Other changes may vary from the need to create to the desire to destroy, from the need to work to the wish to laze. They happen for many reasons, but the Servant need know only that men do change, and how to discern this. Men will often create circumstances to precipitate change, or manufacture incidents after the event to justify their new position.

In the matter of the truth and the perceived truth, there is no single truth about men, but the perceived truth is the operative truth, for this is what people see and believe. What men know and believe about themselves is impossible to tell, but it is probably very distant from the truth: most men will believe what they want to believe. The Servant does not deal with men as they are, but as they think they are. He, on the other hand, has carefully and knowingly constructed a myth for himself. Because it is constructed with great care, the Servant can distinguish between the truth and the myth.

As I have said, there will be occasions, in the service of the Prince and the Idea, when events are so dire that the Servant has to take action that disregards his myth. By doing so he will startle and disturb people who are always angered by inconsistency. Such a change of character may also surprise his enemies, though this must not be relied upon. An avenue of retreat, such as a temporary sickness, must become a component of the myth. This will reveal a human weakness, a quality for which people will have sympathy—as long as the battle is eventually joined and won. When using sickness as an excuse, make it truly revolting. This will be believed and will avoid discussion. Men do not lightly enter into talk of each other's bowels.

The Servant must also embrace the myths of strength and of clemency. These have to be deployed carefully, without showing signs of weakness. In reality, the Servant is ruthless, not letting kindness or consideration enter into his plans. This is the paradox of his position. In the area where the line between the man and the myth is drawn, there can be no blurring of the edges between stealth and action, honesty and cunning, kindness and cruelty, generosity and meanness. Not to draw the line will destroy the concept of the Servant, and unless he is dismissed, he will bring down the Prince.

In the usual course of events one man succeeds another, often someone who has died. Most people respect someone who is dead, even though he was capable of doing them harm and was not popular while he lived. This might appear to be a disadvantage to a Prince and his Servant, but the Servant ensures that the Prince can absorb the respect felt for his predecessor, slowly drawing strength from his popularity while actually consuming it until it seems enclosed by the Prince and his Idea. If this predecessor's popularity was in doubt, the Servant may contrast the Prince's own Idea with it, showing the Prince's Idea to be superior to the actions or policies of his predecessor.

The Servant's dilemma is that he must be feared as a man of authority, while simultaneously he must be loved for the attractive qualities of his person. By love, I mean the love of the populace and not the other, more dangerous emotion that people bestow on others in order to bind them to their own desires and ambitions. I mean respect. The Servant must never believe that anybody really loves or respects him, not even the Prince. All they see and believe is but his myth. All men need reassurance and find public expression of these emotions very attractive. The Servant must, in his own mind, reject the lure of popularity; he is there only to serve the Prince and the Idea. The only publicity sought by the Servant, then, must be for the promotion of his myth, not to acquire the love of the population. He must always remember that he has only one role, that is to serve. His strength and self-respect must come from that, and that alone.

The Servant must, in all things he does, display great confidence; but not arrogance or the sort of presumption that leaves suspicion in men's minds. Privately, he must have no confidence. He must plan carefully, never relying on the promises of others, and his plan must never assume success. There must always be emergency measures to fall back on. The myth of the Servant will differ between those who are close and fear his position, and those who are distant and love and respect him. The latter make their judgements on the smallest amount of evidence. The former, because they are close, are more selective, and may know enough to begin to doubt the myth. The Servant should employ a person to administer discipline among his staff. When this person has become too objectionable, he can be given other duties.

The Servant must be conscious of personal ambition. He knows full well about this, for he is the sort of man who, in any other role, would be consumed by the desire for success. It would be the driving force of his life. His colleagues would admire this ambition, and be jealous of it and, if he failed, they would say of him that he was too ambitious. The Servant must understand that he no longer has an ambition because he has achieved it. By making himself essential to the Prince, he has reached the pinnacle of his career. Since there is nowhere to promote him, he is beyond ambition. The Prince will feel secure because the Servant is not a rival, and when the Idea begins to prosper it will be to their mutual benefit.

Nonetheless, ambition can prove troublesome. The Prince will be treated by people as a prince, while the Servant will be treated as a servant. The Servant will be tempted to use his skill to prove to these people that he is really the equal of a Prince. This is one of the tests of a Servant, for he must be satisfied by the knowledge that he is part of a trinity, and ignore those who would make trouble. The Servant must never indulge in petty actions to prove his status. He needs all the qualities of the ambitious—the driving force and the courage—but must never demonstrate that he has fulfilled his goal. The Servant himself knows this. There is no need for anyone else to know.

It is the job of the Servant to be the Praetorian Guard of the Prince, to be always alert. He will have time for pleasure, but will take his pleasure in activities where he meets men who can be of help to him in his task, for he must devote every hour to the Prince. Only by keeping constantly in mind the Idea of the Prince can the Servant perform his task. He must have his own network of informants and men who will assist him. He must always know how to use the network of the state. Since this network is unlikely to be loyal to the Prince, it must be used with great care, and never trusted.

Information must be gathered by employing a large number of skilled men to assemble background information on a wide variety of subjects. The Servant should thus always be able to make an informed judgement as to the likely turn of events. The Servant listens to many men, weighing their words before reaching his own conclusion. Paid informers must never be used; if by chance the Servant comes across a seller of information, he should be listened to and paid for his services, but these men should never be sought out. Men who sell information for money, ambition or revenge must never be believed in total, although there is an element of truth in every lie, and the best lies are often based on the truth. The words of honest men should always be respected but not totally believed either, for honest men often exaggerate to lend credibility to their truths. The question for the Servant is not whether the messenger is reliable, but who has sent the message, and why. Stupid men are the most dangerous because they may try to make a message more interesting, and they will deliver it incorrectly, causing confusion. The Servant must listen to idle gossip, taking a word from here and picking a word from there, always checking, always looking for a pattern.

The Prince must always be seen to keep faith. This is a very difficult task to perform and may not always be possible, but since the Prince and the Idea are the same, the Idea can only be damaged by any duplicity. There are, therefore, two possibilities: firstly, the Servant tries to prevent the Prince making promises that he may find difficult to keep; the second is that, in the event of a pledge being broken, the Servant must arrange for someone else to take the blame. It makes no difference whether the Servant himself is honest or dishonest, although the myth must suggest honesty. The Servant must be able to change quickly, or quicker than events. When setting out on a strategy of deceit, he must choose very carefully who he will deceive, for while honest men will see the Servant as honest, a deceitful man will spot the Servant's deceit. It is in the nature of men, when looking at others, to see themselves, and apply their own values. Dealing in deceit, as the Servant must, great caution is required. The Servant should know the difference between large and small deceits. Avoid small deceits: like barnacles on the bottom of a ship, they build up in the minds of people whom you may need to convince in a large deceit, making the task harder, sometimes impossible. Avoid deceit when possible—let men deceive themselves, for usually they will believe what they choose to believe. Show them only an easy way, an option that will enhance their prestige and their wealth, and most men will invent their own deceits. Honest men are more difficult, but many of them would rather avoid the issue. They do not need to be deceived, only shown a reason for looking the other way. But beware the exceptional man, the man of conviction, for he could be a Prince.

While the Servant and those close to the Prince will be motivated by the Prince's Idea, others will be moved only by reward. The Servant must ensure that the further these men are from the Prince, the greater their opportunity for reward is, for they are capable of weakening the Idea. From time to time it is the Servant's job to indicate to certain distant but key figures that there is a chance of plunder, so that they continue to work hard for the Prince.

Princes, like many other people, do not like advice unless it coincides with their own thoughts. If the Servant anticipates the Prince's wishes and advises him accordingly, he becomes just another flatterer, an ornament in a court. If you wish to win his respect, do not advise the Prince; make yourself indispensable instead. Seek to remove trivial problems, help him avoid more serious problems. Never ask for guidance. Princes have enough decisions to make already. Never draw his attention to the fact that you perform this role. He will notice. A Prince badly in need of advice is not one to serve. The success of the Servant lies in his choice of Prince; he must choose carefully his Prince. It is the only choice he makes.

What the Prince needs is evidence on which to make decisions. It is the job of the Servant to provide it. In assessing the Prince's judgement, there is a single criterion: does the Prince have all the evidence, and does the Servant know everything that the Prince knows? The Servant never disagrees, just provides the missing evidence. It is, of course, the Servant who grades the worth of the evidence.

The Servant will never acknowledge that his judgement is better than that of the Prince. If the Prince makes a mistake and events prove the Servant's judgement to have been right, the Servant should say nothing. An unwise Servant who gave advice which led to a mistake would damage his position; a Servant who gave correct advice that was neglected would find his relationship with the Prince damaged. If the mistake is fatal, all is lost; if it is only a setback, then the Servant must help to recover the situation. Since he gave no advice, his capacity to serve will be undamaged. If the Prince is continually making mistakes, this is not the Prince to serve, for it seems that he was never truly a Prince. The Prince is not to blame, however, if the Servant foresaw a mistake, and by exercising influence could have stopped it and did not. If the Servant cannot influence without advising, he is a failure as a Servant. If these mistakes eventually cause the Prince to fall, this is an indication of the Servant's lack of ability to serve, support and guide the Prince.

It is the balance of trust between the Prince and his Servant that will make their partnership flourish or founder, and this subtle balance is most likely to be affected by small events. The control of this balance is the job of the Servant. The Servant must be capable of independent thought. It is important for the Prince to know this, but equally vital that the Servant never exhibits his independence of thought on issues of wider policy.

Here the Servant never needs to exercise independent thought, for he must serve only the Idea.

Princes are impressed by wealth. They conclude from the fact that the Servant has wealth that he is clever and that he could leave when he disagreed with them. They will also believe that if the Servant has wealth, he is likely to be honest and not to steal. The Prince will also conclude that the Servant is lucky, and above all else Princes like to be served by lucky men. Because the Prince must not believe the Servant to be extremely clever, far better that he believes him to be lucky.

The Servant must be well travelled, so when foreign places are discussed he can provide background information. He must know many people, particularly the Prince's political contemporaries.★ He must take a deep interest in the minutiae of their lives, again to give background information. He must be cunning, but never plot. His private life does not have to be straightforward, though it is preferable that he conforms to the morals of the age. Those who would attack a Prince through the morals of his Servant expose their hand to little purpose because, to serve well, the Servant must always recognize that he is dispensable in the service of the Prince. It is preferable that the Servant appears to live an open life and allows his failings to be well known. These are part of his myth, so that if they are attacked, they are not a shock to anyone. And being part of his myth, they can easily be got rid of. Bachelors make better Servants because they have more time, and their actions are not influenced by their wives. It helps if his contemporaries think a Servant is lazy, amiable and not too clever. A fullness of figure

---

★ *Editor:* Such a one was Sir Charles Powell, who served Margaret Thatcher in her later years in Downing Street.

helps sustain this disguise. The Prince will see through it. With the Prince the Servant must be amusing, so that he will wish to have his Servant constantly near him.

The Servant must display his wealth to the Prince with prudence, and should never let the Prince see his home. When Cardinal Wolsey and Fouquet, both men of wealth and taste, did this, the result was disaster. In both cases the Prince that they served became extremely jealous. In the case of Cardinal Wolsey, his Prince believed that he could have afforded such magnificence only by dishonesty, and that such dishonesty must be to the Prince's disadvantage. In fact he believed that his Servant had at best used his name to rob others, at worst robbed him personally. This suspicion terminated their relationship, or at least it gave the Prince the chance to rid himself of one who perhaps had grown too close. In the case of Fouquet, his Prince threw him into jail charged with dishonesty; perhaps his real reason was jealousy of Fouquet's mansion, Vaux le Vicomte, even though this Prince built Versailles and is remembered as the Sun King. All those who have visited Vaux le Vicomte will recall the great good taste of Fouquet, but in the end that was his downfall. The Servant must never outshine the Prince. Only the Idea can compete with the Prince, and so the myth of the Servant must be a humble myth. The Servant is content with this humble myth, for he knows the true greatness of service is made all the greater by the importance of the Prince. The Servant must gain nothing from his service. There must be no suggestion that the Servant profits from his employment; unlike morality, this could bring down both the Servant and the Prince. Let this wealth of yours be part of the myth, a demonstration of a style of life. Be not rich if the Prince sees you as poor; appear not poor if the Prince believes you rich.

The Servant should use a little of his wealth to pay a few retainers. These are his own appointments, and not an extension of the patronage of the state or his master. These men should be retired from the game of politics, drawn from the press or party, but not the machinery of state. They will be grateful to be involved at all, and not ask too high a reward. These men are the Servant's tentacles, and will provide the first warning of an attack. They must not be relied upon for defence, but only to serve as warning posts.

The Servant will see that the Prince has enough money to fight battles, though this must be dedicated to fighting his own battles, not those of the people who provided the money.* The Servant must prevent the Prince from becoming a mercenary. Of course, it is true that the money for war must be raised in peacetime. When he need offer his supporters nothing but his friendship, then the Prince is truly a Prince. But men often wish to exact a price from a Prince who is under threat.

The dilemma facing the Servant is that the people who pay to meet Princes are not the sort of people that Princes should meet.† This is where the Servant's knowledge of commerce is useful. A Servant who, although practised in the art of service, is a failure in the world of business, brings with him the wrong connections and is likely to be brought down, or at least brought into disrepute. Nor is it the job of a Servant to suggest to a Prince who he should associate with; this is part of a Prince's judgement. The Servant's role is to make certain people available to the Prince. If the Prince likes their company, so much the better. The identity of these people will depend on why the Servant

---

* *Editor:* This is a reference to party political funding.
† *Editor:* This is a reference to the late Princess Diana and the cult of the British Royal Family raising money for charity by selling their presence at functions.

wishes them to meet the Prince, whether for information, for advice or for pleasure. They must stick to their role. If they move out of it, they must be separated from the Prince. The Servant must never do this himself, but there are various techniques, such as alerting one of the Prince's advisers on to whose ground this person has strayed. His jealousy aroused, the adviser will do the rest.

The Servant must be totally ruthless, even if he prefers his myth to suggest that he is not. He carries out the wishes of the Prince; he has none of his own. The Servant's power is the power of his personality. He must be able to persuade people to take actions against their will, and must have the tenacity to see that they carry them out. On no account should the Servant threaten them with the power of the state. The power of the state and the wrath of the Prince are the Prince's prerogative, and only his.

The Servant I describe is unusual as Servants go. He is not simply hired or fired. He is not employed for just one purpose. He does not stay on when masters change, nor does he leave on a whim, for personal reasons, or for other trivia. People who do these things can be intermittently useful to a Prince, but I write of a man of business, a true Servant, a man close to the Prince and yet distant, a man to be used, but used only with care. The man of business is the confidential Servant, always in possession of information that could destroy his master. Yet the Servant can never use this knowledge to further his ambitions. To do so would force the Prince to destroy him, for the delicate balance between the Prince and the Servant would be upset. Never threaten Princes. The Servant may think like a Prince, but never act like one. Servants do not stand for election; they are appointed by their master, they serve only him. In defeat they follow that master and work for his return. The Servant owes responsibility only to his Prince and the Prince's

Idea; to the state the Servant owes nothing, for the state will only benefit from the success of the Prince's Idea. The responsibility of the state is the Prince's burden, and the Servant makes no judgement in this matter. Once committed, the Servant must carry out only the Prince's will, regardless of his own view.

Machiavelli said that the trouble with Servants (whom he described as mercenaries) is that they are lazy and dangerous. Their laziness occurs when they do not wish to fight, and the danger stems from their ambition. The Servant can overcome the first part of this indictment by diligence. In politics the greatest talent is stamina; the ability to be there, to attend, because to be available at the right moment means being there at all the moments; the habit of attending endless boring meetings, being there at the beginning, waiting until the end, being there at all times, being always available. The Prince, though, will judge the Servant lazy only if he fails. In success, laziness is irrelevant. As for courage in the face of an enemy, who knows who has that? In a crisis, the Servant must carry out the Prince's instructions to the letter. Independent thought is not called for in a crisis; it can unbalance a plan and in these circumstances prove totally disastrous. The Servant has no other role at these times but to be the arm of his master. Other members of the court, relatives, princelings, friends, clowns, dressers, spokesmen and petty officials, imagine that they are there to help, and often try to do so without the knowledge of the Prince. This is the real danger, for if these courtiers have talent, their actions will be uncoordinated and competitive, and if they are fools, they will confuse the Prince, especially if they unwittingly chance upon the right course of action.

Machiavelli's observation that the talent of hirelings might make them dangerous must be taken very seriously by the

Servant, for again it touches on the possibility of jealousy. It is always possible for the Prince to become jealous of a successful Servant. The Servant can overcome this danger by presenting himself to the Prince as a specialist, appearing to be expert in one major area in order to have access to the Prince's thoughts on many other subjects. But in order to remain close to the Prince, the Servant must also be adept at fulfilling a thousand small tasks, because small needs are frequent.

In order to establish in the Prince's mind that the Servant is a specialist, it is important for him to comment only on his subject, and to assert, when asked of other matters, 'I know too little to be of help.' The parafanatics of the court (those who are fanatical about the paraphernalia of the court, men who invest all their energies in insisting upon the observance of protocol, men who care not who the Prince is, being interested only in presence and position and not the Idea) will give advice on any matter. The Prince, seeing the Servant's limitations and knowing his own supreme talent (for he is a Prince), will not fear the Servant as a rival or feel jealousy towards him. The parafanatics will not try to destroy the Servant, for he does not compete for the Prince's ear against their desires or advice. These other advisers are more often interested in giving advice than in carrying through the actions that flow from it. Eventually, the constant Servant is in a position to influence the Prince on subjects on which he says he knows too little to be of help.

The Servant must be very careful not to form alliances in the name of the Prince. Only the Prince himself may make these connections, and, however tempting an alliance may seem, the Servant must avoid this. To make an alliance is to incur a debt that may become embarrassing to repay, for, if the Prince does not do so, it will weaken both the Servant and the Prince.

Better not to create opportunities for men who may become enemies. These men should have honour heaped on them, for this will discredit them among their fellows. Whatever they think of the Prince, it is hard to criticize a generous nature. These men, if they do criticize the Prince after they have accepted his generosity, will lack credibility with all except the Prince's bitterest enemies.

The Servant knows that he will have no reward and that in the end he will sacrifice himself for his master. That *is* his reward, and that is the nature of the Servant. But on leaving the Prince, other members of the staff must be highly rewarded. Indeed, in the view of others, they should be too highly rewarded. This will please them, and they will speak well of the Prince, although this should not be counted on, and it will cause others to be jealous of them, and ensure that they cannot rally support against the Prince should their loyalty fail. The scale of their reward will encourage their successors.

In a true Servant there is no discontent. A disgruntled Servant should not even begin to serve the Prince, for it is from service that the Servant draws his pride (although this pride must remain hidden). When the Prince gives the Servant a task, it is for him to carry it out without hesitation. Should anything go wrong, the Servant will take the blame. When it goes right, the Prince will receive the praise.

The Servant does not even think about a plan until he is certain of the Prince's wishes. Since Princes seldom give direct instructions, it is vital that the Servant is in total sympathy with the Prince, for he must be able to read his mind. Great Princes like to plan great strategies, but they do not like to be asked to make small decisions. When the Servant is sure of the Prince's intentions, he should plan quickly and act with speed. Never hesitate, for even Princes are indiscreet. Never even conceive a plan till it is needed: even as you read the Prince's mind, others will be watching you. If you already have a plan in mind, it can be betrayed by decisions you make that are influenced by knowledge you have and others do not.

The Prince will make only one judgement: 'Did you succeed?' If 'Yes', expect no reward. If 'No', you misread his mind and may have to be sacrificed. Princes come to power in a variety of ways. If your Prince has been brought to power by others who are unknown to you, those who did not get the positions that they sought will seethe with disappointment. The Servant must sympathize with them and extend just a little hope. To those who are chosen, he should fire their ambition slightly, always recalling that success comes only from the Prince. The Servant will find out about the Prince's appointments a little in advance and speak to the recipients in such a way that, when they hear the news, they will believe that since the Servant knew these things already he must have had a hand in them.

The Prince will try to balance the power among his followers; the Servant should never seek to unbalance it.

The Prince can also be brought to power by others, out of revenge. These plotters are going to expect him to be 'their' Prince. This is, of course, not possible. A true Prince is accountable to his Idea and to the people who follow his Idea, *not* to miscellaneous conspirators. In time, these frustrated people will try to overthrow the Prince, for they will have used him to remove a Prince that they did not care for and now wish to have a Prince who will carry out only their ideas. If they do not succeed, they will turn on the Servant. Like angry animals they will seek revenge; all the actions of the Prince will be blamed on the Servant, and these people will call for his dismissal. The dismissal of the Servant is the first step towards the dismissal of the Prince and the destruction of the Idea. In the meantime, the Servant must get to know them well, smile at them and accumulate information about them.

The Servant must also see that none of their assistants occupies any role in the Prince's party. These people have to be removed slowly, in advance of an attack on the Prince. Do not underestimate the role of the minor figures: the Servant must always remember that men will sacrifice more for revenge than they will for gain. The Servant must see that the Prince does not casually put them into a position where they can exact the desired revenge. They are frustrated and must be heaped with honour and wealth (though not power), so that when they attack the Prince, they are seen by the population to be graceless. But these are supposed to be the Prince's friends. What of his known political enemies?

Besides the entrenched opposition, there are the supporters of other Princes who may be persuaded to share the Idea. The Servant must detach as many of them as he can. The Prince must never alter his Idea, for it is the currency of his office, but the Servant can present it in a way that will appeal to these men because they are essentially mercenaries. Once detached, they may be used, but never relied on.

But if the Servant is able to move a man from entrenched opposition to the Prince's Idea, to support the Prince in his Idea, this is a prize indeed. I speak later about converts in general, but occasionally one or two of these converts should be given high office, for he can never return from whence he came and will therefore be secure and loyal to the Prince, until he has some new Idea to follow. These men must not be neglected.

Both the Prince and the Servant have a role in the business of winning new supporters. The Prince expresses the Idea and the Servant promotes it. All Servants have rivals, and they will take care that, in eliminating a rival, the power of another is not increased, or a new threat established. When a rival rises in the Prince's favour, the Servant ought to take a relaxed view; events are never as serious as they seem. Tread with care. Do not enter into battle with this rival; the Servant must repudiate jealousy; there is always the chance of losing much for only a little gain. If this rival has to be dealt with, always remember that all rivals have rivals of their own. Suggest quietly to one of these that he may care to deal with his rival.

The Prince must never be asked to fight the Servant's battles; indeed, it is best if the Servant does not fight his own battles. He must find others to fight his battles for him. Should a number of rivals combine to attack the Servant, this is a different matter, for this amounts to an attack on the Prince himself. This must be brought swiftly to his notice, for he needs to know of the danger to himself. This is a battle that the Prince will fight, for it is in truth his own battle.

In the early days of the Prince's rule, the Servant should indicate his support for the old order in his party or faction. This will infuriate certain radicals and cause them to join his rivals. They will then try to overcome the Servant; the old order will join the fight on the Servant's side, for they hate these radicals. Curtailing the activities of the radicals is useful to the Prince too, for, helpful as they may have been, he now governs all the people, and any elaboration of the Idea must be done by him, and him alone. The Prince will resent radicals advancing the Idea for their own purposes.

When the Prince is established, the old order must disappear gradually, for fear it compromise the Idea by watering it down. Some of the radicals must be encouraged to return to the fold, and become supporters again, believing that the Prince has by now developed his Idea to their satisfaction. The role of these selected radicals changes over time. To begin with, they will have joined with the old order to destroy the rivals of the Prince and the Servant; then, as the old order seems still to hold too much power, they will ally with the Prince finally to destroy it. The new order thus created soon becomes the old order.

Sometimes the Servant will have served the Prince before he attained his rank. It is in the nature of some Princes to want grander men as their Servants when they come to power. Some actually worry about Servants who knew them in humbler times. In early days the Servant must move carefully, indicating how his prestige increases with that of the Prince. Yet the Servant must not allow his myth to become too grand; the Servant himself is far from grand.

As the Prince will have need of company, the Servant may arrange for the great people of the last regime to be introduced. These grandees who formerly opposed the Prince should be used to ornament the Prince's court, without ever being seen as ornaments. Their advice should be often sought, and the Servant must indicate to the world that their advice is always taken by the Prince. In fact the Prince should never take their advice, but since it has been given privately and its content is known only to the Prince and the ornament in question, no one else will know whether it has been followed or not. But these ornaments, hearing that the Prince always takes their advice, will be flattered and believe that he has. So pleased will they be, that they will tell everyone that the Prince follows their advice, and will be seen to be allies of the Prince. But the Servant will know the truth.

When the Prince comes to power, he will find that powerful groups of men who believed that they were responsible for getting him there now expect him to rule according to their instructions. The Prince must find a way to deal with these men, and with their policies, for both are serious matters. Men can be removed only by promotion: their lot must be improved. There is no single way to deal with these people. Some may undergo a conversion. These men are reliable for the moment, as they have nowhere to go. But over time beware these men, they are unsteady, they could become the Prince's strongest critic. Having nothing but the Idea, they feel a passion for it, and perhaps jealousy of the Prince whose Idea it is. Maybe it is better to introduce other passions into the lives of these men. The Servant must reflect on this; some will be promoted to positions of great honour and little consequence; some will have to be sent off to do other work (the Servant must find occupations for them). The removal of these men from any influence on the Idea is essential; only those who truly believe in it must be allowed near the Idea. The Servant is the guardian of the Idea; the Prince invents and propagates the Idea. During this period, the Servant's job is to see that the Prince is not bothered by trivia.

This is the time when the Prince sets the style for his whole rule. He comes under great pressure to change the Idea. He will be tempted to please both those that remain from old regimes and also the population. He will be offered many easy alternatives to the Idea, and many good reasons for adopting them, and he will not find it hard to persuade himself that courses other than the one he has chosen are best. As it succeeds the Idea will, of course, evolve—what sort of an idea would it be if it did not? One doomed to failure. But it will evolve as events evolve, change slowly to deal with circumstances that have occurred, and in this world of truth and perceived truth the Idea should change only according to the truth. The Idea must not be changed according to the views of those who would use it for convenience, people who would change the Idea for they fear this and they fear that. There must be good reason and good evidence for considering the adaptation of the Idea; the Idea must not be changed lightly, and the guardians of the Idea must be determined men.

Moreover, having won power, the Prince will wish to enjoy it and to have no unpleasantness around him. The Prince will be subjected to many trivial pleasures; societies previously closed to him will be opened, he will be in a position to help those that he has always shown an interest in. Beware of this, Servant, and direct the Prince to serious matters, dealing with these trivialities yourself. Jealousy is the danger that comes with new favourites; if there is to be jealousy it must be blamed on the Servant, not on the Prince; the Servant, using his myth, knows how to avoid this blame. But the Prince has not gained power for its own sake. He has gained power to implement the Idea, and the Servant's job is to help in the implementation of the Idea. The Servant must encourage him to stick firmly to it. He will play no active part in deciding how to deal with the great matters of policy, although he will take a keen interest in observing who does.

When the new Prince comes to power, the Servant should act as if the Prince always had it. Because Princes, whether elected or hereditary, have an inborn capacity to govern. It is the quality that the Servant chooses to follow. It is important that the Prince knows this.

I have spoken before of senior officials who help the Prince to power and expect employment. Now I speak of smaller figures. Some will receive jobs, while some will be disappointed. The Servant invents roles for these minor figures, because the Prince has no time to consider them, and they cannot recommend themselves. These lesser figures, while they are no threat to the Prince, could cause the Servant trouble and thus hinder his ability to serve the Prince. He should find positions for these small men outside the world of politics, among the many jobs that are in the gift of the Prince and his followers.

The Servant will find them jobs with small salaries and great prestige: in the world of the arts, for example, or among the many committees of the great institutions of the state. Small men, such as writers of popular books or tunes, may be allowed to attend upon the Prince, since they will amuse him. That is their talent, and it is most unlikely that they would be chosen to replace the Servant, so he need have no fear of them. These small men often have great conceit, particularly the writers of popular books. Their own ambition knowing no bounds, these men believe the Servant's role to be a humble role; they believe that the Servant is merely one who fetches and carries for a Prince. They have no understanding of the grandeur of service, and cannot see that serving a great Prince is a role that gives great personal satisfaction. They seek jobs far greater than that of the Servant, and the spectacle is very humorous. These men seek fame for themselves, and have no interest in the Prince beyond this. These men would not know an idea if they lived for a millennium, far less discover one for themselves. These men seek only grand roles with grand titles so that all will see how grand they are, and even then they will pretend to be grander still. These men are fools: all courts must have fools, and their folly must be encouraged by the Servant. The Prince will believe that the things they say are to entertain him, for no sane man would believe them to be true. These foolish men can be extremely useful for they like to talk at length, and their talking can occupy the time of the Prince, empty time that might otherwise be filled by troublemakers. These foolish men are entertainment, and exist only to entertain.

After this first period of his rule, the Prince tires of this amusement, and such people will fade. The Servant will be secure again, without having had the trouble of removing these people himself, and without the irritation that might have been caused should they have been removed roughly.

Machiavelli observes that Princes, especially new ones, tend to find more loyalty among those men whom they originally distrusted than among those whom they trusted. The Idea converts enemies into allies, and by rewarding these converts the Prince encourages others. It is true that the whole point of politics is to change men's minds, and as I have said a few of these men are suitable for high office—but it is doubtful, although they show the true zeal of converts, whether they can be trusted fully. True, they cannot return whence they came; they cannot be rivals. It would seem therefore that, in general, they are the ideal courtiers. But it must never be forgotten that they have been political enemies and may, in time, turn dangerous again for any one of a thousand irrational reasons. However they may rationalize their change, the fact that they made it in the first place shows them to be irrational and so dangerous. The Servant must find other matters to fill the minds of these men. Never allow them to become courtiers; ensure their lives are occupied with other activities so that they will have no desire to be courtiers. For such converts must not feel the frustration of isolation from the Prince and the Idea, both of whom they now love. These are dangerous men.

As to the treatment of the loyal old supporters, it is not in the nature of the Prince to neglect them. If they begin to fail due to an inability to adapt to the Prince in power, he will simply shift their functions to someone else, while leaving them with the title and all the trappings of the job. The Prince will continue to praise them, and the Servant will go on encouraging them.

The servants of former leaders must be treated with respect and, although they have failed, they must be promoted. This makes them useless to their former employers, who will be jealous of them. The Prince should never feel the need to destroy a former leader's servants, or even former leaders themselves. Always offer promotion: deal more than generously with former leader's servants and former leaders, for if they reject the promotion that is offered and that promotion is seen to be generous, then they will be regarded as churlish, and do what they will, say what they will, thus treated there is no possibility that they can blame the Idea or the Prince.

The Prince destroys old ideas with his Idea. Former leaders must be given great honour and raised above the battle. Having grown accustomed to this style of life, they will not risk it for the sake of younger men and frustrated men who work on new ideas. Let these former Princes continue to preach the defeated idea. If you leave an old cockerel in a pen of chickens, you will not get many fertile eggs. He may have become infertile, but the young cocks are still no match for him. Better still, the radical young men will be discouraged by the former leaders and their servants who are now enjoying these honours. It makes current allies out of former rivals. There is little danger in the defeated idea, but great menace in a new idea. Let the old ideas suffocate new ideas. The Prince should not allow himself to be blamed for resisting the new men and their idea. By doing so, the Prince will only draw attention to their virtues.

The Servant must cut off any avenue of retreat for the supporters of the Prince, committing them utterly to the Idea. The Servant must also see that there is nowhere for the Prince to go should he be tempted to leave his Idea. The Prince must stay with his Idea, and any retreat from it alters his relationship with the Servant and destroys the point of this relationship. The Idea, having grown stronger because of its consistency, will attract supporters and, when it comes under attack, they will defend it.

The Idea will also attract supporters who, while not particularly caring for the Idea itself, so dislike the opponents who are attacking the Prince that they support his Idea. These men must be watched, for when times are hard they will advise that compromise is necessary. There is no harm in adjusting the empirics of the Idea, but the Idea, although it can evolve, must never be changed for convenience. If they are taken seriously, all will be lost, forever. There will be times when the Prince is very unpopular. The Servant must encourage the Prince to reaffirm his Idea at these moments, for popularity is never universal or constant. The Prince's Idea is not about popularity; the Servant must always remember that the population distrust change, and to change the Idea at a moment of crisis, even if it were momentarily sensible to do so, would prove fatal, even if this course of action did succeed. If the Prince survives only by weakening his Idea, by trimming or compromising around the edges of the Idea, or by actions of convenience, he will as surely bring down the Idea as if he had torn out its heart.

When the regime changes, it is vital that all the old retainers of that regime are dealt with honourably. This costs the new Prince nothing, although it does make the beneficiaries the objects of the jealousy of his own supporters. Consequently, a Prince must not take them into his confidence, because this will unsettle his supporters. They must be honoured publicly and cast out in private, so that when they complain, as they will, they seem ungracious. If you propose to destroy a possible enemy, do so by promoting him.

The Servant, on his appointment, will find himself very busy. Nonetheless, time must be made for those who helped him achieve his position, even if they personally oppose the Prince. It is only by continuing goodwill from all sides that the Servant will be useful to the Prince. In his promotion, the

Servant must be careful to take no action that could destroy his myth; he must continue to appear to be the same man.

Machiavelli instructs us that men ought either to be well treated or crushed, because they can avenge themselves of lighter injuries, but not of more serious ones. A good Servant will reflect carefully on this advice and then ignore it, for the Servant's power, although wide-ranging, is to deflect, not to destroy. A Servant persuades. Ideally, he never needs to demonstrate his power. The Servant encourages the promotion of his enemies, allowing the promotion to cause their destruction. If by some chance they avoid destruction, their promotion will have removed them from the path that the Servant intends to follow. No man with Machiavelli's philosophy can be employed by a Prince for anything other than carrying out assassinations, after which he must himself be removed.

A Servant must organize his affairs so that there is time to travel throughout the land and consolidate distant friendships. People in faraway provinces may have power far in excess of their seeming importance. Often they feel neglected. It is not enough to bring them to the capital. By visiting them in their own lands, their greatness is exhibited to friends and acquaintances in their hometowns. Never underestimate their pride or their conceit. Men in the regions are always jealous of colleagues from the capital.

There are certain jobs over which the Servant will have an element of direct control. Since it is not wise to fill them with acquaintances, friends, relatives, or strangers, the choice is very difficult. The best-equipped people for these jobs are people who have retired, but they are seldom acceptable, often being said to be too old. So the Servant is forced to choose between the four categories. First he should appoint his relatives. Although these can be as treacherous as anyone else, in the last resort there are other pressures that can keep them under control. If there are no relatives available, the Servant should make the appointments on merit. Never give jobs to friends: they make the most dangerous enemies. Strangers can be useful, and the fact that a man is unknown to the Servant can be a positive advantage, for he can introduce him to new contacts.

The Servant must beware when the Prince wishes to appoint his own relatives. Tread like a cat where the Prince's relatives are concerned. Genius does not run in the blood. Servant, always remember that a Prince will value blood above all, whether he be elected or hereditary. This is part of him; it involves his virility and his conceit. You are dealing with a living manifestation of the Prince's humanity, of his pride. Have as little to do with his heirs as possible. They may have influence with the Prince, but to use them as tools is too risky. Smile at them, bow to them, never criticize when they have committed a folly. Although his fury is originally directed at his child, the Prince may, with time, redirect it at the Servant. The wise Servant will have nothing to do with the relatives of the Prince.

The Servant's public posture must always be against change. It is in all this that the Servant finds his myth most useful. Always appear to support the old order, and be seen to be conventional. The Servant must never redecorate his office on coming to power; never even rearrange the furniture; no new carpets, no new pictures. He must wear the image of his own predecessor like a glove, but he must also remember that it is his hand inside the glove. The Idea must be radical, but its implementation must be carried out as if no small thing will change. When changes are suggested, never oppose them, but never support them vigorously. The Servant's private position is to support only those reforms demanded by the Idea and necessary to strengthen the Prince's position. The Servant must discover unseen ways to

pour adrenalin into the bloodstream of bureaucracy. The reputation of a rival can be damaged by remarks such as, 'He is a fine
man, he believes so strongly in change.'

The Prince may wish to introduce reforms for no better
reason than a feeling of confidence. The Servant must beware of
this: it is the big dipper of fame. Reforms must be undertaken if
the Idea requires them. Be very careful of your involvement in
the Prince's desire for extra reforms. Nonetheless, the Servant
must carry out his will, and it is inevitable that he will make enemies in doing so. Note their names and watch them always.
The Idea of the Prince will require the institution of reforms;
once these have been carried out, the success of the nation
makes further reform unnecessary. The Servant when faced
with the danger of casual reform must assess the profit and loss
after the Prince has decided on his course, and cause this balance
to be shown to the Prince. He must not persuade him to change
his mind. Of course, the Servant must, under no circumstances,
try to frustrate the Prince: the Idea is the Prince's Idea. If the
Idea calls for reform, then there must be reform—in this area
it is the Idea that is paramount; it is not the job of the Servant to
inhibit the Prince. If the evolution of the Idea needs to be
speeded up, the change in it coming suddenly, then this must
happen. The Servant can only warn the Prince of what many
believe to be the consequences of these actions.

The Servant must be liberal with hospitality; he must show
a generous spirit but have a reputation for shrewdness with
money. It helps to come from Scotland since people assume this
of those who come from that country—and people like nothing
more than to believe their prejudices. The Servant must nurture
this part of the myth. An ability to raise funds for the benefit of
the Prince is of the utmost importance. In the matter of raising
money, his ability can be measured exactly by the Prince; no

myth can save the Servant here. While cultivating this reputation for generosity, a Servant must be careful not to stray into magnificence. Princes can be critical of the lifestyle of their Servants.

The Servant must be careful with his own funds, for if he were to waste them, he might be driven to dishonesty, or, almost as base, be accused of it. Such an accusation would involve him in a battle which would be a waste of his time, would make the Prince suspicious, and might even bring them both down. The Servant must live within his means, drawing satisfaction only from his work. The Servant must live with style, but this can be done without ever competing with the men of substance. (Note that they will tend to hide their wealth when the Servant comes visiting, lest he should ask them to support the Prince more generously than they have already done.) The Servant must reward smaller supporters out of proportion to their worth. This will make a large impression on them, and they will tell of the Servant's generosity, while richer men talk only of their own. The Servant must take care to see that small men who work for the Prince are well rewarded. The Servant must never be seen to waste the funds of either the Prince or his subjects. Important people are irrelevant in this context, for they are paid in a different coin of far greater value. The Servant may spend small sums from the Prince's funds to reward originality, using these grants to encourage certain groups favourable to the Prince. These funds can become a source of envy, and many people like to have the patronage involved in their distribution. But funds are for winning support, not for the self-promotion of other individuals, and it is the job of the Servant to see that they are used this way.

The Servant understands the social uses of wealth, knowing how to give small amounts to charities, and how, by spending this money, to set up a social web. The Servant knows his wealth is one of his credentials, for people will categorize him immediately if he has money, and this will be to his advantage.

Money can be used wisely, or offensively. The Servant must never believe that because an individual may be offended at receiving money he cannot be bought. The Servant must deal in people, buying and selling them at their own price and in their own currency. It is from having money that some men draw their status, but money alone only gives them power over weaker men. Other men use money to give them true freedom: the ability to choose. The Servant would be wrong to assume, however, that a man who has money has no other talent, for the reverse is likely to be true. The Servant's talent is to understand the employment of funds so that the effect they have will multiply. Should one of these successful men learn the Servant's trade, he could be extremely formidable. Certain individuals feel a need to know people who have money. Others need to reject money, while still using it. Money can be used by the Servant crudely, to buy things, but mostly he deals in persuading people to do things for the Prince, so the Servant must know how to use money to influence them. The Servant must understand the power of money in other people's eyes. To them money is like a standard that they carry before them. The Servant has no use for money personally; it is only because others believe that money has some real value that the Servant can use it as a means of influence.

The Servant should not acquire property. Having done so he will be disliked by his tenants and his colleagues. Property is too obvious a sign of wealth. It is the same with companies. Having bought them, to make them work he will sometimes have to take stern measures, and consequently will be disliked. Why should the Servant involve himself in these areas of risk? The investments of the Servant must be secret and small in volume. Small investments in a variety of undertakings, placed to give the Servant patronage, are a cheap and very effective way to be popular.

Should the Prince find himself in the wilderness, he will probably be poor. It is the job of the Servant to see to his needs. The Prince, unless he is to retire (when it is best if he too goes to the country and takes up agriculture), must always beware of action that would prejudice his return to power. The Prince must under no circumstances engage in commerce: it is not that the Prince might involve himself in any transaction that would mean that blame could at a later date be attached to him, but that the Prince, being unfamiliar with commerce, might innocently involve himself with those who would undertake such transactions. Those who are Princes, those who will be Princes, and those who have been Princes, must avoid commerce. The raising of money must be left entirely to the Servant, who can be sacrificed in the event of trouble.

When a Prince is in the wilderness, the systems of the State that supported him before will be gone; it is the job of the Servant to see that these are replaced, and that these replacements are independent of vested interests. There are those who, wishing the Prince well, will say, 'Come, join my empire. I will provide for you.' This is not acceptable, for the Prince is a true Prince, not the client Prince of anyone. The Prince must always conduct himself in a way that leaves open the possibility of a return to power. The period in the wilderness must be blameless. The Prince must spend all his time furthering the Idea. The Prince must have the time, the place and the funds to regenerate the Idea, for his enemies will try to destroy the Idea while the Prince is out of power, believing wrongly that in this way they can destroy the Prince. The Servant must gather round the Prince people who supported the Idea. These must be people of intellect whose minds can help the Idea and whose voices can promote it. The Servant must see that the Prince does not waste time on useless undertakings, that he spends no time with those who would waste his time, for in this period when the Prince does not govern he has no need to talk to those who are not his trusted supporters. The Prince must spend all his time preparing the Idea and himself for the future. The Servant has nothing to do with the Idea: he spends all his time in seeing to the needs of the Prince. Among these needs is the promotion of the Prince's own myth. The Servant must travel, tell all of the greatness, the kindness and other attributes of the Prince. The Servant must tell these things in such a way that his hearers will repeat them; the Servant must spend time building the myth of the Prince (for the Prince in the wilderness has need of a myth). The Servant also builds his own myth; the very act of creating a myth is a very important lesson in deception. When telling these things he may use humour, for he needs to be sure that his sayings are repeated. A Servant will, as he creates his myth, use a variety of images. As opposed to the myth, which comprises that which is reported to the Servant, an image is what is actually seen or heard of the Servant. The Servant will not manufacture an image whole and new, but will use a series of images that exist already and combine them so they become uniquely his—for instance, by continually smoking cigars, always the same size and always the same make; by attending the opera regularly and always occupying the same seat; by using the same restaurant, always sitting at the same table; by attending the same night club on regular occasions between the same hours. The use of shorthand in creating an image will help the Servant—for example, even though the Servant will be a member of many clubs, he wears always the same club tie, since people will be aware of the significance of the club, its members, and the type of person likely to be a member. The Servant will attend the football matches of a favourite team, go to the horse races, always wear similar suits and shoes. In this way, the Servant can always be found by those who would seek him out, and recognized by those who do not know him. He will seem to be predictable, a quality people find reassuring.

Each of the images the Servant adopts will signal a particular reaction in other people. The Servant must choose each of these images with great care, for they will influence the public view of his character. The Servant must exhibit these images regularly, so that the public identify these images with him, and only him. To change an image will worry the public, and must usually be avoided. The Servant modifies his appearance only to signal a change in his own attitude to events. Using his carefully constructed collection of images as part of the myth which is his shield and disguise, the Servant may still manoeuvre outside his myth and these images, though this must be done secretly. The Servant must be known to always be at certain places at certain times, so that other men may be able to meet him there should they wish to tell him something. They will know that they meet there on purpose, but will believe the Servant to be unaware of this. The Servant must also be aware that, having created the belief that he will regularly attend certain places, should he fail to attend, people will place greater emphasis on the Servant's absence than may be justified. So the Servant, having created an image, must stick to it. This is why he must never take up an image lightly. Creating images can be exciting and entertaining in itself. A man of imagination will find toying with images a seductive alternative to the boredom of an orderly life. The Servant must never fall into the trap of using an image to impress friends (male or female, particularly not female), colleagues or the public. The image must always be complementary and part of the Servant's myth. The image is to be used only to serve the Idea and the Prince.

The Servant must learn not to believe his own publicity. He must also see that the Prince does not believe it either. It is better if the Prince does not read newspapers, for they only say what the Prince's friends wish him to hear or what the Prince's enemies wish the population to believe. They are not suitable evidence to make decisions on; the Prince, being well served, will be informed of events that occur.

Timing is crucial, and must be carefully studied. When something objectionable has to be done, the Servant will want as little public reaction as possible. He needs to study the logistics of the media. The Servant needs to choose a day when there is plenty of other news, for it is better that the Servant's bad news competes for a place to be reported. He may even find it convenient to create other news at that time, as a diversion. The Servant must also consider the time of year; he may choose a time when many people are away. Also he should never tell a writer anything except to influence him. He must be discreet but appear free with information. If you wish a fact to be repeated, make it interesting or humorous. If you wish that fact to remain hidden when questioned about it, make it sound extremely boring. If these rules are followed carefully, it should be possible for the Servant to take objectionable action without too much trouble. The Servant then uses the myth to cover his tracks. The Servant is known by his myth, and it is by his myth that men will judge him. They might say, 'He could not have done such and such; he tells me all that he does, and he said nothing of this.' Or, 'That is totally out of character—the Servant could not have done that.' Even, 'The Servant travels each summer; he was not here.' 'He has no interest in that subject; why would he do that?'

The publication of books must only be for a purpose. Most people do not understand what they read; they glance at the words, then form opinions. The Prince takes a great risk in writing books. A Prince's political memoirs, or even biographies of him, give opponents the opportunity to comment on his performance. Most people read book reviews rather than the books themselves, and since reviews are often written by people hostile to the Prince, these can be very damaging. They can give the impression of opinion forming against the Prince.

The Servant never accompanies the Prince to the theatre, lest he laugh in the wrong place and the Prince misunderstand his attitude, for the Servant, while not agreeing with the playwright, may still find a satirical reference very funny. Princes do not find being mocked at all funny.

Incidentally, the Servant should never forget the power of the political cartoonists. They should be cultivated by the Servant, and he should occasionally be pictured in their work, for to be occasionally an object of fun is useful to the Servant. It will cause those around the Prince to see him as a less serious figure. The Servant should cause the work of the cartoonists who feature the Prince in a kindly light to be bought, thus encouraging them to continue to do so. Humour is the polish that gives a shine to the Servant's myth. Remember, though, that there is no force so terrible in politics as humour. Never, in jest, say anything that may when repeated interfere with the myth, although jesting is a way of building a myth, for men love to repeat jokes. The use of humour is not to be overlooked, but it must be used very carefully. It is, for example, useful in the destruction of an enemy. Never use a joke unless you intend to.

It is sometimes sensible to try to alter the course of a disaster by trying to turn it into a farce, although only as a last resort. Normally humour is far too unreliable, but it can be used to tell of events without seeming to do so. Humour can be a destroyer, too, but only after careful consideration. Casual jokes must never be used. The funnier the joke, the greater its currency. But, in the course of time, the victim will hear the joke and never forgive the Servant, becoming a dangerous and unnecessary enemy.

Humour can be used by writers to reveal a deeper and unspoken truth, but never, ever, make jokes about a victim. Humour and jokes are not at all the same thing. Enemies can be destroyed slowly with humour. Humour is a slow-acting poison; with time a man can be made to look foolish and of no ability. The joke is the axe, quick and effective. To ridicule another man with a joke is to invite lasting enmity; to be humorous about yourself is to invite affection.

To think in politics is dangerous. To react is less trouble, but unsatisfactory. What has happened has happened. To be instinctive is a problem because it involves the future. To think about the past or the future can endanger the Idea. The Idea must be the touchstone, the guide in all situations.

The Servant ought to beware of men of intellect. They deal in theory. The Servant deals in reality. However much he may be attracted by theory, it is reality that will shape events; he starts with situations not as they were years ago, or will be centuries in the future, but as they are on this day. Then he can arrange the public's perception of them to suit his purpose. This does not mean that the Servant should not mix with intellectuals. Quite the reverse: he must meet and debate with them as often as possible to sharpen his mind, for without constant debate minds quickly go blunt.

I have advised against plotting. Now I will go further. Never plot with the Prince; never tell him of cunning plans to overthrow those who rule in other countries. He must think of these schemes himself. In any court there are people who will urge the ruler to strike down some other ruler, but he must never think of the Servant as a plotter. When the Prince has decided to plot, show him only that you can carry out his wishes efficiently. Fewer men can carry out plots than can concoct them. There is a vital rule to the execution of a plot: credit for it must never be attributed to the Prince or to his Servant, especially if the plot succeeds.

In failure, the Servant has to be quick on his feet. A measure of confusion is the best tactic: total confusion even better. The Servant's myth can be called upon to spread uncertainty. At the worst, the Servant must take the blame. As for success, it is always easy to find someone to take the credit, for the desire to succeed, and to be seen to succeed, is among the greatest of human failings. The Servant's successes must be secret. Every public success makes the next task harder. For example, he may have cultivated a particular high official; this official should not be encouraged to greet the Servant with a kiss, while merely waving at others. This will enrage rivals and they will identify in their jealousy a plot, or see a plan where there is none. There is no sensation so infectious to an alert observer as the current that passes between two men who share a plot. Never forget that the Servant moves in a world of alert observers.

The Servant must never be seen to execute a plot. It is his job to convey the sorrow of the Prince to victims of the plot, to lay the blame broadly, and to offer help in their adversity to those who have been overthrown. The Servant must spread stories of the Prince's generosity, for the wise Prince never claims victories as a result of a plot. It has succeeded if his enemies discover that their plans have been set back. The Servant views the outcome with the appearance of sadness, especially if an idle courtier takes credit for the plot himself. As for the victim of a plot, he must be found an occupation quickly where his new colleagues will be keen that he does not bring them all into disrepute by speaking ill of the Prince.

The Servant will dine with the Prince from time to time and when he does so, he should never raise serious matters. He should be humorous at meals, he should have a light touch with the Prince, using humour, not making jokes. The Servant must ensure that the Prince knows that he will never press him with difficult questions, for the Prince knows well that these difficult questions have to be answered, and he will not care to have to give that answer as he eats. The Prince will not invite a man to dine with him often who disrupts the Prince's dining. It is possible that the Prince may raise a serious matter; only then does the Servant speak seriously. The reasons for dining with the Prince are fourfold: first, always to be available to be asked any serious question; the second, to collect the trivia about the court and the Prince; third, to let others know that he dines with the Prince; and fourth, to listen to what those others who dine with the Prince have to say.

The Servant must never try to advise the Prince who he should or should not see: influence should only be brought to bear on which people get to see the Prince. It is the power of access that is the real power: it is difficult to influence a Prince you cannot see, or see at the wrong moment. By far the best form of access is when the Prince travels. The Servant should always travel with people he wishes to lobby.

In politics, access is the most vital factor. However much people plot and plan, they can be brought to nothing by access. It is important that the Servant identifies and gets to know all the minor officials in the departments of the grand officials with whom he has dealings. For instance, the office of the

Prince may be controlled by a relatively minor official or chief-of-staff. While the chief-of-staff must never appreciate that he personally is not being cultivated, do not waste any time on this man. Real power is in the hands of the keeper of the diary.

Access can be used in two ways: either to allow a man to put a plan to the Prince, or to stop him from doing so. This process is conducted not by forbidding the man to see the Prince, rather by arranging appointments at a time when the Prince is either too busy or has spare time, depending on the desired result. It is foolish to bring a complicated issue to a Prince in a hurry. This makes it unnecessary ever to forbid appointments to people anxious to see the Prince.

Access can be used to destroy or advance; for advancement it is clearly necessary to choose the right time for the man who is to be advanced to see the Prince. And the right mood. Not so much the mood of the Prince: rather, it is important for the Servant to get the man he wishes to advance into the right mood to impress the Prince. But the Servant can also destroy a man by arranging access at the wrong time. The time when the Prince has other matters on his mind or is in a hurry to leave for an appointment to which he has been looking forward, this is a particularly deadly time, for the Prince will be in a good humour when he greets his visitor, and this visitor with his time-wasting rubbish will spoil a day that the Prince thought he was going to enjoy, so it is unlikely that the Prince will be keen to see this visitor again. This is a certain way to ensure that the Prince is not impressed with the man. Or maybe the Servant can wait until the Prince is deep in conversation, and then suggest that this person should interrupt, telling him that the Prince is keen to have his views on foreign policy, or the rating system. This has an additional advantage because the victim is left with the impression that the Servant has done him a favour.

A man who argues intelligently is hard to deal with in this way. The Servant must have prepared the Prince to receive such a man, giving the Prince information to construct arguments to counter those of the intelligent man. He may not be an enemy of the Servant or Prince; his arguments may turn out to be extremely helpful, or if not he must be destroyed by promotion. But he must not, under any circumstances, be ignored by the Prince or frustrated by the Servant.

Another use of access to destroy is to invite a man to put a plan to the Prince when the Servant knows in advance that he will disapprove. This will damage the man in the Prince's estimation. The danger of access is that people will often say more than they intended, and so set off unpredictable trains of thought in the Prince. The Servant must judge carefully the amount of time that a man needs to deliver his message: short messages need only a short space of time, and even if the messenger is a friend of the Servant he must be allowed only a few minutes. He must not be allowed time to spoil a good case. If he is a friend of the Prince this is even more important. The Servant must be alert to this risk and be skilled in bringing an interview to an end. The Servant must also ensure that there is time for himself to meet with the Prince, for Princes can often become overwhelmed by the affairs of state, seeing only representatives of other nations, leaving little time for their own Servants.

In this matter of meetings, the Servant must be a master mechanic. In meetings he keeps silent. What needs to be done must have been dealt with before the meeting begins. Most of the statements made at meetings are repetitive, people saying the same things in different ways, each one trying to take the credit for the original statement.

If the Servant has arranged things well, someone else will always say what he has in mind, and he can remain silent as long as his aims are being achieved, for the Servant goes to a meeting to achieve an end, not to demonstrate his cleverness. Sometimes, a meeting will begin to go off course, and then the Servant will have to speak. First he picks on an inaccuracy made by some minor figure. By savaging him, he ensures that he is listened to at meetings.

The Servant chooses the minor figure because it is easier to win the argument. More important, as the Servant will have to make his peace with him later, this minor figure may very well come to hold the Servant in high regard: the minor figure will be content with a small benefice or even a few kind words. Major figures do not like to be savaged in front of their colleagues—it might well cost the Servant much to repair the damage. In argument, should it eventually become necessary, the Servant should start by agreeing with people's beliefs, only gradually changing his view from theirs to his, at the same time carrying them with him. The Servant never argues for pleasure.

It is virtually impossible to implement any action in anything like its original form after a lengthy debate. There will always be compromisers, and, given the nature of any debate, they are likely to win. This is particularly true of a public debate, where these compromisers can pose as moderates, when in reality they are men without any very firm commitment. If something objectionable must be done, it should be done without the benefit of debate.

The Servant must never allow secret meetings to take place in his home, or any other property he may own. The risk is that the outcome of secret meetings will draw attention to him. These meetings will always be tagged with the name of the place where they were held. This will always be an embarrassment to the Servant, since it always brings his home to the mind of the Prince whenever a disastrous meeting is recalled, especially as the Servant's enemies will take care to mention it.

It is the job of the Servant, however, to provide places for these meetings and he can, if these meetings are successful, always choose a name for them that will be to his advantage. There are many men who would seek a place in history. Name a meeting after one of them. They will readily lend a house and pay for the privilege of doing the Servant favours. It is strange, this desire of men to be remembered. Name a dish by a famous chef after one of your guests, let him see it on the menu in a popular restaurant—you cannot imagine the man's delight.

The Servant must be skilled in the use of language. For example, he will leave a word hanging. He rehearses this, carefully choosing the word that he will throw into the conversation. The idea is to nudge the talk in the right direction. Do not spell things out. The politician will use a phrase repeatedly; he will take three arguments and discard two, repeating the third three times, for the audience does not hear it at once, and the second time does not properly understand. The politician works with repetition and emphasis. The Servant, who is not a politician and must never imagine that he is, works not through repetition, but through suggestion, and he uses only the subtlest forms of suggestion. Now it might be said that this technique could never penetrate the barrage of words that comes from politicians. This is why the ground must be carefully prepared, so that when politicians do hear a suggestion they will seize it for their own, repeating it endlessly.

The Servant must be adept at the drafting of documents, for he will appreciate the power of words. By his choice of words, he is able to persuade, which is a far more powerful weapon than force. The Servant must often practise this. When he starts to persuade, the Servant will use the same technique as when he argues. He will agree with his opponent and slowly change his opponent's view, moving gradually from position to position, always agreeing with him, and displaying a detachment from the Servant's own stated views. Sometimes, the Servant will even criticize his own opinions, but always he draws the views of his opponent closer to his own—until the opponent discovers that he is, after all, an ally of the Servant, and will do his bidding.

It is worth noting that the agreements reached at most meetings are based on a mutual misunderstanding of those agreements but, as time will pass before they are implemented, this does not matter. By then one side or the other will have become the more powerful, and their views will prevail. Moreover, many of the clauses people wish to have in documents are of no account, for they are there to cover all eventualities; in politics this is not necessary as time moves very quickly. In the art of negotiation, it is important to give way quickly on a few small items. The Servant will agree to anything, provided he knows it cannot happen, and he will always be prepared to retreat from his views and agree with an opponent provided he is confident that he is able to reverse the result of that agreement at a later date.

In argument the Servant usually tries to elevate the tone, only putting people down when it is absolutely necessary, and then only very occasionally. He will make his opponents feels better for losing by taking their reasoning, extending it until it appears ridiculous, and then laughing before admitting that he is wrong. The Servant tries never to ridicule and cause one man to laugh at another. He laughs only at himself. Nobody who negotiates with the Servant must feel bitterness. In argument he will use pathos, in such a way that the opponent does not know whether to laugh or to cry. Then the Servant will play on his opponent's emotions in the least expected way. Here words must be chosen with care. The Servant fits the words to the situation, using a short word if there is only time for a short word. Timing is of vital importance to the argument. Use a long word as you would use a pause, and use a long word for effect, but never too many. When the Servant wishes the opponent to speak, he will fall silent, for men find it hard not to fill a silence with their words. If the Servant remains silent for long enough, the opponent will say something he had no intention of saying. This is a case of leaving silences for fools to talk into. The Servant never uses words the opponent cannot understand. He avoids this apparent advantage, for in reality it makes his opponent feel inadequate, and therefore wary. The Servant must also be careful of bringing new facts into the argument, since their impact can be unpredictable. He argues along the lines that he has planned.

The Servant must be skilled in interpreting documents. He must fully understand the meaning of words and also appreciate that words do not always mean what they were intended to mean. The Servant must also be skilled in adjusting the meaning of words and follow the advice of Humpty Dumpty: 'Words mean what I wish them to mean and, if I use them often, I pay them overtime.' (The Servant never hesitates to borrow a phrase from a man of greater talent.)

The Servant must know men who understand words and men who understand policy. These will be different men, for they are different trades. The Servant must also know men who are skilled in the selling of words once they have been written, for this is yet another trade. The Servant must be certain that each of these skilled operators practise only their own trade for, inevitably, each of them will long to practise the other's. When words are written by them, they must be the Prince's words, reflecting the Idea in every respect.

The Servant must see that the Prince is not swayed in this matter by clever words for, in the world of politics, if an action seems to be clever, or if it is to be taken because it is convenient, it is likely to be wrong. Politics is about simplicity and the future, and the real art of politics is about surviving long enough to implement the Idea. For the Prince and the Servant and the Idea, short-term gain is of no advantage. It is of no interest to them just to govern. The ground must be prepared to receive the Idea, for they are interested in governing only according to the Idea; merely occupying a job has no appeal to them. The Prince and the Servant will use images, the myth and any other means to achieve this.

The messenger of a Prince is a man of great power. A messenger bearing a message to the Prince is in great danger. Who knows how it will be received? Never be the bearer of bad news. The Servant has to see that the Prince's messages are delivered as they were intended. It is easy for a messenger to deliver the same words in many different ways so that, for example, angry words seem soft to the recipient. The messenger will always be tempted to alter the emphasis of words to deter wrath or to increase his own prestige. The words of the Prince must be delivered as they were sent. There must be no misunderstanding. Use no more words than are necessary to make their meaning known.

It is better that the messenger is unfamiliar with the events that surround a message, since he is less likely to place his own interpretation on it. Never let men deliver a message who have been involved in the policy in question, or men who could benefit or, worst of all, forget a part of it. The best messengers are distant from the Prince, but known to the Servant.

Monuments must always be large and preferably very ugly. They should be built to commemorate past regimes; people will recognize their ugliness and resent them. Always promote past regimes; show them to be powerful, for this enhances the prestige of the Prince, since they are gone and he rules. Accord them plenty of glory, for there is no harm in this. Beware of shrines, such as a spot on the pavement where people commemorate a potent cause with flowers. These shrines are extremely dangerous, especially when they are in open spaces where people can gather. Praise the cause, and gain the sympathy of the people. Agree that flowers should be laid, but say that there is a need for a greater monument on this spot; replace the simple shrine with a very large complex for public use, named after the cause of the shrine. Fill the space so that people no longer meet there. Build extravagance where there once was simplicity and the cause of the shrine will lose support. The sponsors of the shrine will find it hard to oppose the generosity of the Prince, both in terms of money and his attitude to the enemy. The people, really preferring a useful building to a shrine, will support the Prince.

The Servant should persuade the Prince to erect many statues, particularly to the heroes of his opponents. These should be erected where they interrupt the flow of traffic, or cut off a favourite pedestrian path, so that the public will react against them. In time they can be pulled down with public approval. The building of such statues is how the Servant deals with the image of the Prince's opponents: he promotes them to a position that is ludicrous.

While learning his trade, the Servant must travel. By visiting other cities he learns the feel of greatness, and begins to understand the use of monuments, for they are the impedimenta of history. Furthermore, the Prince may call on him to deliver messages to foreign rulers and it is as well to know the people to whom they are to be delivered, for it may be that the Prince needs the help of foreign friends to support and promote him. It is also useful for the Servant to be in a position to recommend the Prince's messenger to them. The assistants of these friends must be known to the Prince's Servant. It is always important for the Servant to make contacts with men before they rise to fame. Many will achieve nothing, but those who do will know the Servant is not interested in them only because of their fame. (The Servant must never stress the fact that he knew them before they were famous since they may not recognize a time when they were unknown.)

I have used the word 'man' in the old-fashioned sense, but not through any belief that only men are capable of operating in the world of Princes. Indeed, there are many women who play quite as significant a role as men. I use 'man' simply because I dislike the words that have been invented to cover both sexes at their work. So calling all those in active politics 'men', I would now like to refer to those involved on the periphery as 'women', for that is mainly what they are.★ The Servant must be friendly with many of these women, entertaining them often, taking trouble to win their goodwill.

The Servant would do well to operate through these women, using them to gather and pass information. It is important that they are never given the feeling that they are being used. Rather, they should always feel that they are being useful. The desire to be useful is very strong; the pleasure at being included in a secret is very great; the urge to be party to a seeming plot is irresistible. The Servant will find no shortage of women to help him, and many men will listen to these women, and, out of conceit, will tell them many things which they, from excitement, will repeat to the Servant.

The advantage of these women is that while they are outside politics and affairs of state, they meet regularly with others who

---

★ *Editor:* Regardless of their actual sex.

are greatly involved in both. These people can be very useful to the Servant for delivering his messages, apparently impartially, or indeed unawares. They are good at passing information for they love to talk, although they often do not know the significance of what they say. Conversely, the Servant must always beware of women who may be used as traps by his enemies.

The Servant appreciates the need for care in the matter of sex. He will listen to women and pay much attention to what they say, for this is what they enjoy most. When listening, the Servant is not telling, and by not telling, remains secure. Many of the great Servants have worked through women, for they attend parties and have time to move around society and politics and in and out of houses where they hear a great deal. One of the great Servants in recent times, by chance a woman, employed men for this purpose, but men are often suspicious of other men. Women will not suspect the Servant, particularly if he listens carefully to their talk.

As for sex, the Servant must have none of it, never lusting after the women of others. This excites jealousy and all sorts of other, less predictable, adventures. Never pursue women. Apart from anything else, men will boast about the pursuit and this is a great danger, both because of the indiscretion itself, and because boasting is a habit more easily acquired than lost. Being a man of supreme imagination, the Servant will meet a better class of women in his dreams, and these women come when the mind calls and go at its command, silently, telling nothing.*

As I have said, the Servant sacrifices all for the Prince and the Idea. He must give up all his own ideas to concentrate on his

---

* *Editor:* This was written at a time when the British Conservative Party was beginning to be beset with a series of scandals, most of these sexual. As a result, that party was about totally destroyed at the polls in 1997.

task, but it is vital that the Servant moves in society. He must attend the opera, parties, everywhere that people gather, for he must always be listening for information and spreading goodwill for the Prince. The way that these people view the Servant is very important. The Servant must have a working knowledge of the arts, literature and sport, for he must seem at home at these gatherings. He must never claim great knowledge of these subjects, only an interest in them. If he claims knowledge that he does not possess in these matters he will easily be found out and so allow himself to become despised, which would greatly damage his value to the Prince. He must be discreet, giving just enough information to make his company sought after. He will always say that he knows no secrets because people will believe the opposite. This is as it should be, because the Servant must never leave the impression that he is kept in ignorance on any matter. If there is a subject about which discretion does not allow him to reveal even one small piece of news, it should not be discussed at all; for in revealing small pieces of news to an alert listener he risks revealing all. It can be perilous for the Servant to mislead people; they do not like it and they will grow to mistrust him. The Servant's myth must be that of an honest and interesting person. He should never imagine that he will make friends by telling secrets. The Servant must say nothing in confidence. Confidence does not exist.

The Servant must suggest to the Prince that he entertains, and let everyone know how much the Prince likes to entertain. The Servant must be responsible for these entertainments and will see that, though the banquets are large, for many people must be entertained and none must be left out, they are none the less modest. The Servant will use this as evidence of the Prince's generosity and his modesty. The choice of food and drink at these entertainments is a matter of careful judgement.

The Servant himself also entertains, but on a much smaller scale, and in an intimate manner. He serves only the best food and drink, for these will attract people to his table from whom he can learn much and who he can, in turn, influence. There are few people so important that they will turn down an invitation to dine where the host employs a great chef. The Servant must employ the greatest chef and maintain a brilliant wine cellar. It is very important that he is known for both these things.

At functions attended by the Prince, the Servant should, when appropriate, be there as well, watching from a distance to see if he can be of help. The Servant must not engage the Prince in conversation. The object is for the Prince to meet other people, not to take up his time talking to the Servant, which only causes envy and annoyance to the others at the function. The Servant must ensure that he is seen once by the Prince. This is called 'being seen by the widow', after the practice at Jewish funerals. The Servant may be tempted to introduce someone to the Prince whom he feels he ought to meet. He must resist the temptation. The ground must be carefully prepared for all introductions, and an introduction to a Prince is too serious a business to be risked at a party. Many men at parties will try to meet the Prince. Those whom the Servant would introduce must be of use to the Prince and the Idea.

The Servant should have many casual friends who will speak well of him. They will praise him to the Prince in the hope that this will improve their own position, and the Prince will understand the praise for what it is. But some of it will stick, and improve the position of the Servant. But he should never rely on his friends. His only deep relationship is with the Prince and the Idea.

Machiavelli is of the opinion that Princes should be protected from flatterers. This is wrong. Flattery will stimulate the Prince and is better for him than alcohol. Princes need flattery to encourage them, on occasions to raise their spirits, and as long as they truly know the nature of flattery (and the Prince will certainly know that) there is no harm in it. The Servant should beware those men whose honest intention is to tell the Prince 'the truth', for they repeat only their own opinions or their own view of events, and such opinions are worth only as much as the men who give them. Indeed, these opinions are worth less than those who offer them, if that is possible. Although these men may be sincere, their opinions will be coloured by their own interests. The Prince, on the other hand, has to make a decision in his interest and in the interest of the Idea, and his judgement must not be coloured by the likes and dislikes, anger, fear and greed of others. The Servant should encourage flatterers and discourage those prophets of gloom who are just as likely to be wrong in their judgements as the tellers of truth. Right or wrong, they will depress the Prince. The Servant must beware the reaction of the Prince to these prophets of doom: the desire to avoid all men and all advice and, in time, all news.

An able flatterer is a useful man at court, for if he is good at his job, he will be seen for what he is and no danger will come of it. The flattery of enemies must be examined with great attention, for in their flattery they can reveal secrets. The Prince should listen to these enemies, but must not be deceived by their goodwill. When he receives this goodwill, which is a reflection of his own success, he must use it, but it is vital that he does not believe it. Should a policy fail, the Servant will find that his enemies have predicted it. His job is to transform their predictions so they look like support, by recalling selective quotations from their earlier flattery.

At times the Prince may need to be reassured, may truly need flattery, and then it is the job of the Servant to see that he gets it. It will do no harm for, as I have said, flattery will not alter the judgement of the Prince. The Prince must see many people and hear all manner of things. Princes do not need to be told of their mistakes. There is nothing more annoying than to be told that you are wrong when you know it already. It is important that the Prince enjoys flattery and fully understands its value. A Servant must ensure that the Prince has time to listen to other men; this will flatter them. There are many reasons why the Prince will listen, and few of them are for enlightenment. Only a bad Prince tries to be the same as his followers. Men like to be led by a Prince. Indeed, many men want to be Princes themselves. Men will not want to be with a Prince who spends his whole time doing as others wish. If he wishes to flatter, the Prince must listen to these men, who will tell him he is a Prince, and then how he should behave. The Prince will know that they can never be the Prince themselves.

About these people who press their company on the Prince: never warn him against them individually. Rely on technicalities and the jealousy of colleagues to see that their views do not prosper. The Prince, like most humans, can tire of fellow human beings, and the Servant must watch for this, constantly placing the person he wishes to destroy in the path of the Prince until the Prince begins to ask what he is doing there. At that point the Servant may, just by chance, fail to find a convincing explanation of that man's role.

Machiavelli says that by acquiring the love of the population, the Prince will prevent them plotting against him. But it is not the population that does the plotting. Plots are hatched by senior officials and colleagues of the Prince. Plots are seldom hatched successfully by his avowed enemies. The views of the population only provide the ammunition for these plots, and these views are only what clever plotters would have them be. Plotters will say 'the people believe this, or believe that', but the people are mostly unaware that their desires are being used to further a plot. Those who claim to express the desires of the people are reluctant to ask the people publicly to express themselves. They claim to act on behalf of the people, but they do so with no mandate.

The Servant must take the view that his colleagues will plot against the Prince all the time, even if they do so only in their minds. Grand officials will either agree with the Prince's Idea, in which case they will try to steal it, or they will disagree with the Idea, in which case they will try to destroy it. The Prince must not concern himself with plots or plotters. The population has no interest in plots.

The Prince's enemies and the enemies of the Idea will plot to turn the will of the people against him, and the Servant will counter this not by cunning, but by the strength of the Prince's Idea. The Servant cannot rely on the love of colleagues or the observations of petty officials to warn him of attack, so he must constantly be aware of the meetings of the Prince's colleagues. As plots are secret, plotters will meet privately to avoid discovery by the Servant. The Servant must constantly monitor the places people frequent, and if the Prince's colleagues are not to be found there, he must wonder why. Most plotting is done in the homes of the plotters and therefore remains secret. The Servant must never tell the Prince of these plots, for to tell him would not, in the end, promote the Servant's cause, or further the power of the Idea. The Servant must know of them only to give the correct evidence to the Prince when he has to take action.

Machiavelli gives several examples of complicated plots: of Annibale Bentivogli, for example, who, as Prince of Bologna, was murdered by the Canneschi. He tells how the people then rose and killed the Canneschi, so great was their love of Annibale Bentivogli. It could be that Annibale Bentivogli was murdered by

another party, whose aim was to put the blame on the Canneschi. In a democracy, murder is not a practical political tool,
but it is realistic to plan to shift the blame, marshalling the anger
of the population to destroy an enemy who played no part at all
in the plot. It is always hard to get to the bottom of a plot, to
find out who really should be blamed. Do not waste time on
this exercise. It does not matter. All those involved share the
blame in one way or another.

Machiavelli remarks that individuals must never be annoyed
but utterly destroyed. Individuals can be destroyed by the device
of encouraging them to behave like nobles for, although there is
still a certain amount of respect for the nobility, officials, both
grand and small, are jealous of newly ennobled figures. The
greater the apparent prestige of these people, the less their real
influence with the Prince, or, for that matter, anyone else. In
order to destroy, promote as high as possible. Promotion to a
second chamber is one way. Many men who are prepared to
honour the man who has been promoted will resent the thought
that his heirs, who deserve no honour, will benefit. Seeing these
heirs promoted above them, they will be deeply jealous and
work against the recipient of the honour, where before they
were indifferent.* For those engaged in these affairs lack generosity of spirit. They do not realize how little consequence
their spite is to the Prince and the Idea. The Servant must never
be spiteful and must never allow himself to deal in actions or
thoughts that come from spite.

Having encouraged a man to behave like a noble, a hint to his
colleagues that it would not be against the Prince's will if he were
destroyed will cause them to tear him apart. This is destruction

---

* *Editor:* Hereditary promotion to the second chamber has only recently been
abolished in Britain.

by elevation, the pulling down of a man by an act of generosity, so achieving the Prince's aim with no blame attaching to the Prince. For the Prince is a generous man who promoted the victim. The blame attaches to the man's rivals, jealous men, envious of his promotion. In the destruction of this man they make themselves vulnerable, and so inhibit their capacity to become powerful. At the same time, the myth of the Servant remains one of nobility.

There are certain areas of public life that are small but vital, like the arts. The Servant must see that the Prince, if he is not interested in the arts himself, appoints someone who understands the working of that world, remembering that the arts are a perfect distraction for a political enemy. They could also be a distraction for the Prince whose job it is to implement an Idea— he should waste no time on them, using them only occasionally for personal pleasure. The political enemy will be occupied fully, for the politics of the arts are far more complex and consume much more time than the politics of ruling whole nations. Those who take up these posts in the arts with enthusiasm are instantly lost to the world of plots and treachery, and their silence is cheaply bought; a few pounds for a favourite opera, or the purchase of a picture by the gallery that they command. There is no possibility of a man building a political base from within the world of the arts, and it makes an excellent parking lot for troublesome politicians. It must be arranged that they are in no position to complain without seeming churlish. The Servant must see that all their vanities are satisfied, and must also ensure that the people observe that these vanities have been satisfied. In reality it is impossible to satisfy their vanities, because these men will always call for more.

Those involved in the arts are extremely dangerous, for they form what was once called 'the chattering classes'. These men have to talk, to talk of a past that was never as they describe, to talk of a future that will never be as they hope, and their words are listened to by those who would direct fashion and presume to form the opinions of the people. The Servant knows that these men are of little account in the matter of achievement, but he also knows that their words count for much among those of their own class, so he must show them deep friendship (this is part of his myth). Moreover, any success that they may achieve does not make them popular, either with the party or the people at large. He must help them in their continued calling for money to promote their own interests and enthusiasms. By their self-seeking actions those in the arts alienate themselves from the citizens, who by contrast are interested first in finding work and then in entertainment, usually of a sort that these men would have only contempt for.

The Servant must never stress how easy it is to get rid of Servants. The Prince already knows this and will think that the Servant feels insecure and is therefore unreliable, and possibly dangerous. Consequently a shrewd Prince would exclude him from his council, and he would become like any other hired servant, of no use to himself or the Prince, or the Idea.

Princes sometimes like to tell secrets. A good Servant will avoid hearing them, especially any secret that, to be kept, ultimately requires the Servant's death. Knowledge of such a secret will always worry the Prince and he will blame himself for telling this important fact to the Servant in the first place. There is no emotion so destructive of the relationship between the Prince and the Servant as the Prince knowing that he has made a mistake. He may forgive the Servant's mistakes, but not his own, ever. The fact is that this secret will in the end destroy the whole scheme of the Prince, the Servant and the Idea. Do not, under any circumstances, accept a secret from a Prince. Secrets are of very little use to a Servant other than to bolster his pride. The information that the Servant needs is a vast quantity of everyday trivia about the Prince's life. With this information, there is no secret at which the Servant cannot guess. The Prince feels secure because his Servant knows no secrets, and the Servant feels secure because he knows all secrets.

There is but one thing to be remembered: that the secret does not exist, nothing is ultimately secret. Secrets recorded in diaries, however long delayed, will eventually become known. The Servant must proceed in his negotiations on the basis that all will at some time be made public. He can, however, assume some flexibility over the timing of this publicity.

The man who would do you a favour is your friend for life. The one who would ask a favour will one day be your enemy. The giving of true friendship is the greatest gift that one man can give another, and he that would give this friendship can always be relied upon. The receiving of favours without bitterness needs a man with a character as generous as the one who would do him the favour. The Servant should always beware of those whom he has helped and rely totally on those who have helped him.

The best advice the Servant can have will come from his enemy for he, if he is competent, will have studied the Servant most closely. A great enemy will have taken the trouble to discover all facets of the Servant's character in order to destroy him. The Servant has created his myth to shield his real character from such an enemy. The truly great enemy may penetrate the Servant's myth. As this enemy acts against the Servant, he will reveal to him weaknesses that the Servant did not know existed; these weaknesses have to be quickly repaired. To be attacked by a great enemy is not always bad. In fact, it is part of the training of the Servant for, should he survive this attack, the

Servant will be better fitted to serve the Prince and the Idea. The Servant need not seek out enemies to attack him as the Prince and the Idea prosper; they will appear, and, because of the experience gained, each one is easier to defeat than the one before. But never become complacent because of the ease with which enemies have been dispatched in the good times. Prepare always for bad times, when conflict with even the smallest of enemies could so weaken the Prince that others, seeing this, attack him and win. Always remember that dragons in shallow water are the sport of shrimps. Small men who openly attack the Prince must be defeated publicly and a great spectacle made of it, to encourage the Prince's followers and to discourage enemies. The small enemy must then be made to appear important in some other occupation, by the means that I have described before. Never fight battles for entertainment.

The Servant knows that a war is not won by a simple victory, or lost, for that matter, by a defeat. Rather, his concern is how the Prince will use that victory or defeat. Therefore the Servant must prepare the Prince for either outcome, allowing neither excessive rejoicing nor despair to affect the final outcome of these wars.

The Servant must prepare the Prince for retreat both physically and mentally, so that he has a strong refuge and a firm will to fight again. He also prepares for victory, so that the Prince does not pay too much attention to it, nor waste time on celebrations, which is what many around him will want. The Servant and the Prince must resist celebrating victories, for out of these celebrations comes only jealousy—it is important when this is done that no one should feel left out. The Prince must continue to carry out his Idea as if this conflict had never taken place. Battles are only distractions and, whichever way they go, they must not be allowed to divert him for long. In defeat or victory the Prince still expresses the Idea, and all that will have changed is that he has either more or less power to promote it.

In the case of elected Princes, elections have to be fought as the Prince would fight a war. He is the general responsible for all things: the Prince appoints, the Prince dismisses. In an election no detail should be left to chance; all decisions must be made by the Prince. Others will imagine that these decisions are theirs, and in peacetime this may be so, but in wars and elections the Prince must decide everything. Fame or blame is his. The Servant must not allow men to believe in false victories: to win is to gain ground and to lose is to retreat. To still hold power yet to be forced to retreat is not a victory—it is better for all men to realize this. The Servant must not encourage the celebration of false victories, for men will conclude that they did well when they really need to alter their style of warfare in order to win in the battles that will surely follow. Always beware complacency; the Servant must review the tactics of battle, improving them constantly and treating even true victories as if they were defeats.

The Servant who understands that an effective means of damaging a rival is to promote him, must beware of those who would promote the Servant's own fame. The Servant must never appear to be powerful. His master must always believe that the Servant has no interest in power and that his interest lies only in service. Generosity and strength of character, weaknesses or ruthlessness may be obscured by the Servant's myth, but not power, and any attempt to promote the Servant's fame must be stopped at once. Efficiency and service are the only qualities that the Prince must see in the Servant. The people, if they are aware of him at all, must see him as human. The Servant must see himself as ruthless. There is no action that the Servant will not take to assist the Prince further the Idea. This sense of purpose is nowhere revealed in the Servant's myth.

The Servant must never be seen to promote the fame of grand figures, for they tend to resent the help of others, however pleased they may appear to be at the time. When these grand figures have their positions improved the Servant will influence these appointments, and if he wishes to assist a colleague, will pass the credit to him. Most people are perfectly happy to take the credit for the promotion of others.

In the case of minor figures who have no other chance for promotion, the Servant must take all credit, even if he had no hand in the matter. This is always possible, because the Servant will have prior knowledge of these appointments. The Servant's myth will be strengthened by his being seen to help these minor figures.

The Servant should occasionally make it his business to reward people who will catch the imagination of the public. To recommend a small medal for a popular entertainer is good for the Prince and costs nothing. It is strange how people love medals, how even those with grand hereditary titles are pleased to wear them. Most men seek rewards that they find hard to achieve, or even rewards that there is no chance of their receiving. This should be encouraged. The Servant must never believe that a man's ambitions have been fulfilled, or that a man is too grand for a flamboyant but small reward.

The Servant should become intimately acquainted with the varieties of revenge. Machiavelli's advice in this matter is good for both the Prince and the Servant: 'When he seizes a state the new ruler ought to determine all the injuries that he will need to inflict. He should inflict them once for all, and not have to renew them every day.' Machiavelli is right: all actions should be taken at once to diminish the power of enemies, but revenge should be used only sparingly, if at all. Revenge should not be used against a fallen enemy; in that case generosity is a more certain weapon. Revenge must be used only by the Prince, and it must be sudden and sure. The Servant's armoury does not contain revenge and his myth contains no hint of revenge. Figures who cross the Servant are cut down by their colleagues. The Servant must always smile goodwill on all. He has no feelings but the feelings of the Prince, and it is only at the bidding of the Prince that these figures find that the tide of life has moved against them. The Servant, like the Prince and the Idea, always moves forward; it is their purpose always to improve; they have no time for, and no interest in, revenge.

I have spoken of how rivals must be dealt with. Now I will discuss how a system of alliances changes after a rival has been removed. Do not assume that because men help the Servant to remove a rival, they do this entirely for his sake. They hope to make a step up for themselves. Today's champion is tomorrow's enemy. The removal of a rival may therefore necessitate the removal of a whole string of rivals, even if this leaves the Servant with a great deal more work to do himself. Consequently, I counsel that the best way of dealing with rivals is to increase the number of their own employees and followers (there are few who can resist the lure of a new assistant), and then to draw this excess to the notice of the Prince. The rival, if he is dismissed, will leave others behind capable of carrying out the work.

Even if he follows these rules, the Servant will always be subject to attack. So let us consider the position of the weakened Servant. Having been driven back, he will have to seek allies. And if he should win, these allies will become his enemies; seeing the Servant remove his enemy, it will occur to them that it may not be hard to remove the Servant. They must be disposed of immediately. This is difficult, and only a

Prince can accomplish it. But if the Servant does not get rid of them, they will feed off him. Indeed, this may be the time for the Servant to publicize his victory and then to retire with honour to take up agriculture, for he can win only a certain number of public battles. The number of private battles that he can win is endless. It is often better for the Servant to leave a tiresome rival in his position, and put up with his attacks, than to destroy him and leave a vacuum for some equally tiresome but unknown rival to fill.

Better for the Servant to avoid a fight, but if he is drawn into one, he must be totally unscrupulous, using all his personal knowledge of his opponents to discredit them. He will set the retired men of good repute on his staff to slander his enemies. Although it is out of their character (this makes the slander more effective), they will do so because without the Servant they are nothing, and the Servant, whom they trust, will suggest words for them to say. Those organizations, clubs, and societies that the Servant has assiduously supported must be turned on the enemies of the Servant. They will provide seemingly neutral opinions. The use of neutral opinions in politics is of the highest importance for it has credibility far beyond what it deserves, as men seldom study the source of independent opinions but always believe them.

The Servant lives with danger, and must constantly be aware of attack. This requires him to be an expert in the area where he wishes to fight, for the Servant must always choose his own ground, ground that he has prepared with many traps for his enemies. He can do this by retreating until he reaches it, so the battle will be well within his capacity. The Servant never fights an offensive battle; his offensives are silent offensives. Since he works through influence, nobody is quite sure if he has won or lost until the result becomes obvious. He must also plan for every eventuality. However many the numbers on the dice, the sum of the numbers made by each throw must benefit the Servant in some way or another.★ But the best defence of all is his myth, which will suggest that he is a harmless figure. Because he is only the Servant, few will waste their time attacking him.

Servants are seldom attacked by the Prince's enemies, but often attacked by those who call themselves the Prince's friends. The Prince's enemies attack only the Prince. The Prince's so-called friends wish to remove the Servant to put a placeman in his job, and so in time bring down the Prince. They are enemies of the Prince, but not worthy of the name of enemies.

I mentioned before how Machiavelli counsels that when a person has to be destroyed, he should be destroyed utterly. This rule should not be applied to organizations, or to the people who run them. Often, when an organization has grown large and exhibits the trappings of power, its idea has in reality grown weak. When the people see a few men enjoying this power and its trappings they find it difficult to believe in the idea, for these men use the organization to improve their lifestyle and are not interested in the idea which originally made the organization powerful. These men are not Princes; these men are not a serious threat, for their idea is in the wilderness, unused, an embarrassment. They must be encouraged in these worthless activities, in the pursuit of greed and self-promotion, for the Servant and the Prince and the Prince's Idea can only benefit from their folly. Now if, as Machiavelli suggests, these men are destroyed, they may well become martyrs, and their idea, freed from their incompetence, will become strong again and may bring down the Prince, the Idea and the Servant too.

★ *Editor:* A reference to the game of dice known as Backgammon.

So there must be no martyrs. Instead, control of these organizations must be relocated, their very purpose for existence changed, and their leaders rendered harmless. Having become dependent on their trappings, these people can be destroyed by removing their paraphernalia. Do not hand this paraphernalia on to anyone else, because in time these people, or others like them, could restore its potency. For instance, their buildings must be torn down, for if they stay intact, they might become shrines. It is always possible that the empty space where once these buildings stood could become a shrine, so the space must have a popular use. In a busy city it might be transformed into a hospital or multistorey car park; in the country, into a building for growing food, the keeping of large numbers of pigs, perhaps housing for chickens and the intensive production of eggs. As I have written, it is difficult to erect or maintain a shrine on ground used for good or mundane purposes.

Without their trappings, opponents will not be able to nurture their idea and it will grow weaker and shrivel. The Servant must turn this to his advantage by seeing that these men continue to control their idea (but not their organizations), for should it fall into the hands of new men, they might revive the rival idea. So the Servant must preserve the original men in control of their idea (thus stifling their idea) for as long as possible. Although these men are beneath the notice of the Prince, and he would tend to neglect them totally, they must be brought to his notice by the Servant, entertained and, as proprietors of their idea, given honour by the Prince. The prestige invested in them will help them survive, and while they hold tight to their withering idea, it is very difficult for young men to prosper with a new idea. The Servant must never leave a vacuum in the world of ideas.

The Servant must understand that a man with nothing to lose is the most dangerous enemy, for he has time and colossal energy. However grand or small this man may be, he is still of very great danger. The Servant must remember that whenever a man is cast down totally, he bears a grudge. The Servant must also remember that the relatives of men who are frustrated in their aims, or cast down, often bear grudges as well. The Servant must prevent him or his relatives from causing trouble by making sure that this man is left with some position that he fears to lose. The role has to be carefully chosen, for under no circumstances must it be a position from which he can recover.

The Servant never corners enemies, especially the smaller ones; he further takes great care that the final dismissal of these small enemies should be delayed (a period of travel, a post overseas). Then, should they go and work for a rival, the information they bear with them about their employment will be long outdated. They must also be given great honour in their going, for it is the situation that people perceive, rather than the reality. If their situation looks better than that of others, it will be difficult for them to get the support of others for their trouble-making.

Great care must be taken in these matters, for the whole system of the Prince, the Idea and the Servant could be brought down by leaving one small man without hope. The small actions are the ones that tend to influence great events—one man and one pistol have changed history. Never neglect details.

Machiavelli talks about the merits of arming the population. In some states citizen have been allowed to carry arms, while in others with conflicting philosophies they have not. There is no rule on this matter, for the ideas of each of these states have in time grown weak. The populations are no longer totally able to believe in them. So should citizens be armed or not? In fact, if they need arms, they will get them. But the Prince must see that his Idea is strong, for while it is, the population will not revolt and there will be no civil war. Only when the Idea becomes cluttered and deteriorates, so that it is merely a vehicle misused by lesser men, will they resort to arms. It is the strength of the Idea that is important to maintain the internal security of a nation. A strong nation will be well able to maintain its external security as suits the age in which it flourishes.

Although the Servant may plan with great care and proceed thoughtfully, one of the many elements which can destroy the best plans is the intelligent subordinate who, having been given an instruction, believes it to be foolish and changes it. Of course it is necessary for the Prince to employ subordinates of intelligence, for to be served by idiots would lead to downfall, and there is little point in telling the subordinate only to carry out instructions. This will inevitably cause antagonism in the subordinate and cause him either to work against the Servant or to leave.

However, it is beyond the capacity of the intelligent subordinate merely to carry out instructions without having his own thoughts about them. The Servant does not want to have to explain his plans, for this will lead to a series of debates and take too long. The Servant has to exercise much patience in the work he does, and none of it ought to be wasted on explanations. Even if the Servant has explained the plan and debated it with an intelligent subordinate, he is still likely to change the plan, making it a worse disaster than he already thinks it is. What does the Servant do? The Servant studies these intelligent subordinates, and considers how they may react to the Servant's plan, and he takes this into account. He will plan and counter-plan, so that if the first plan, being driven off course, founders, there will be another to put in its place.

How does the Servant treat the intelligent subordinate who has done this? The Servant explains his mistake, apologizing for the error of not informing the intelligent subordinate, claiming to have forgotten, and then congratulates him. Thus the Servant will have rebuked the intelligent subordinate, while also having displayed that human weakness which some confuse with humanity. The intelligent subordinate will tell all, helping the myth of the Servant, and enhancing the reputation of the Servant. In time, perhaps, the subordinate may become intelligent enough to obey without question.

It is one of the contradictions of his myth that the Servant, as well as seeming lazy and amiable, will have the reputation for hard work. This is acquired by letting people know the hours he works, for men are much impressed by long hours. They respond to time, not effort. But the Servant must never claim to be too busy, for if he were to do so, people will suggest to the Prince that he needs someone to help him. They would like the Servant always to be under observation, and as the Servant must do many things secretly, he needs nobody to help him. Nor must he have anyone of equal status in his office, only subordinates. To superiors, the Servant is as important or as humble as the occasion demands. The Servant must never allow himself to be allocated a position which defines his status.

The Servant must always give credit to another for his ideas. Firstly, he needs to encourage men to tell him their thoughts, so that he can use them in the service of the Prince. If he is known to steal their talent, they will be reluctant to do this. Secondly, there is nothing that provokes a man to anger so surely as to see another profit from the theft of his own ideas, and the anger of these men is not good for the Prince or for the Servant. Because they have talent, they could endanger the idea. Credit for men of talent must always be great. It will show the Servant's generosity of spirit, an important element in his myth.

The Servant must never try to do everything himself. He must always employ specialists to whom he will give credit for their work. Although, if their work is faulty, it is the Servant who must take the blame, for it is he who chose them.

A Servant must never expect more from people than they are capable of giving. It is important to remember this in the promotion of subordinates, for the Servant will be as strong as the ability of the people who work for him. Therefore, if he has a subordinate who is working well, it is rash to promote him. By doing so the Servant takes two risks. One is that the subordinate may not be as competent in the new job. The other is that the new replacement hired to carry out his former function may fail.

But while some men are content to perform the same task for great lengths of time, the best of them wish to be promoted. How can the Servant deal with this? First, he must, at the right moment, increase the wages of the subordinate, then—again at the right moment—change the title of his job without ever changing his function. Slowly, more responsibility must be given to the subordinate so that he always lives in hope. But the Servant avoids the trap of the sudden promotion, for it tends to lead to arrogance, and dismissal. The Servant must always praise his subordinates, showing kindness in their personal problems, but when they fail, the Servant must be ruthless and they must be made to vanish, to disappear into obscurity, yet feeling only great goodwill towards the Servant.

The Servant must study manners, and by this I do not mean the social graces. The Servant will need to suit his manner to all occasions, and his language too, for it is essential that he is understood; conversations often result in confusion, and the Servant should never assume that he has been understood.

It is possible to tell how a man will act from the manner of his speech. The Servant should learn this, for the manner in which a man orders his words will change as his thoughts change. The Servant will be able to detect the change before the individual concerned knows himself that he is about to change. These changes in men are so important that they cannot be too carefully watched, for it is these changes that unbalance events and bring danger to the Prince. As I have written before, a man whose whole approach to life is about to change will often exhibit this physically; there are telltale signs the Servant must watch for.

To mark a memorable occasion the Prince may desire to offer the Servant a gift and, wishing to be sure that he will enjoy this gift, may enquire what he would like. The choice is important. The value of the gift is no criterion. The only consideration is what gift the Servant should choose so that his choice will raise his standing in the Prince's eyes. He must not be accused of false modesty with a cheap gift, or of greed with an expensive one, of gluttony with food, of drunkenness with wine, of arrogance and ambition with estates, or with the hand of a woman who might create jealousy. No good will come of honours of this kind. The Servant must decide for himself. I only warn him of the danger.

Perhaps the best solution is to ask for something from the hand of the Prince, a speech inscribed, or a piece of philosophy written in the Prince's own hand. This gift combines flattery with economy. But, in future years, this memento could become of great value to the heirs of the Servant. Its worth in the auction rooms of another generation is, of course, dependent on the fame of the Prince, and may prove an additional spur to the Servant's desire for the Prince's success.

The Servant must be careful of very dull people for, although they lack the ingenuity to cause trouble for the Prince, there are many dull jobs to be done, and many dull people to do them. Together they amount to a vast force. They move slowly, they do not plot and plan, they are predictable—and herein lies the first danger. The Servant deals in the unpredictable, in change and in new situations. Dull people, on the other hand, change very slowly, and it is hard to tell when they actually have changed. Moreover, when they do so, because there are many of them, if they begin to reject the Servant and the Prince and the Idea, they can bring down any one of them. They may not know why they reject the Prince and the Idea, they may not even dislike him and his Idea, but politics is about collections of ill-informed opinions moving in one particular direction. It is about misinformation and half-formed judgements produced with certainty; these form waves of opinion that roll towards the beach. The Prince must ride these waves: indeed, his Idea must be the wave he rides. His Idea must become one of these waves but he must remember there is always a wave ahead of him and a wave behind him; he must join these waves with his wave, or the dull people, only half-thinking, will bring him down, for it has always been the tradition of dull people to offer as a sacrifice, their Prince.

There are no devices for controlling dull people. They can be motivated only occasionally by material benefits, more often by a curious sense of right and wrong. These two factors spring from the Idea: if it works, they will benefit materially. When the nation is wealthy these dull people will be calm, but there will be times when it is hard for the nation to achieve wealth. Then only the strongest ideas will survive. While it is taking root, they must feel that the Idea is right, and it is the use of the word 'right' which counts. Although they do not understand the Idea, they will follow what they believe is right. Do not imagine that the minds of dull people can be moved only by money.

Now the opponents of the Idea will try early on to disrupt its course in the hope of destroying it, and they will tell these dull people many reasons why they, too, should oppose it. The dull people will not believe them as long as they believe the Idea to be right. What the Prince and the Servant must do is promote the rightness of the Prince's Idea and make certain that material benefits flow from it before too long. Dull people have brought down rulers often before, and they are conscious of the great power which they can use to support or destroy the Prince; but being dull, they hesitate to use this great power.

As often as not what we call luck is something else, like inattention to detail by an opponent. The Servant eliminates luck as far as possible. He must plan to do without it and see that luck or acts of God do not affect the Idea. Essentially luck is good planning, although there is no point in planning for every eventuality. If it is going to rain, it will rain. Plan to avoid areas where rain matters.

Never neglecting details, the Servant must avoid an obsession with them as he plans. Other men have often said about attention to detail: 'Look after the pennies and the pounds will look after themselves.' It is more true to say: 'Look after the pennies and the pounds will go astray.' It is the overall concept that really matters: if the Idea is strong enough, it can overcome defects of detail. The Servant must never spend too much time on the detail of a strategy. He must plan on the grand scale, constructing his plan on experiences gained from knowledge of how men think and react. The Servant, the Prince, the Idea are nothing if they are not grand.

Having planned the Prince's luck, it must be put to good use. How the Servant chooses this use will be a matter of judgement, and it is by this judgement he will succeed or fail. Should he find that he is having a run of luck, he will begin to worry.

Planned luck is the study of the minutiae of events, something people seldom do. Apparently trivial events have gone by unnoticed and historians—having no explanation for them, or through slackness or the inability to identify what becomes lost with time—call them collectively luck. The Servant must not waste time studying all these minutiae. The practical advice to the Servant is to be well informed, to understand the habits of men, and to assemble a mass of different information; only then may he succeed in eliminating luck.

Machiavelli says: 'I conclude, therefore, that as fortune is changeable whereas men are obstinate in their ways, men prosper so long as fortune and policy are in accord, and when there is a clash they fail. I hold strongly to this: that it is better to be impetuous than circumspect; because fortune is a woman and if she is to be submissive it is necessary to beat and coerce her. Experience shows that she is more often subdued by men who do this than by those who act coldly. Always, being a woman, she favours young men, because they are less circumspect and more ardent, and because they command her with greater audacity.'

This is bad advice for the Prince and the Servant (and certainly as a method of dealing with women). It is evidence of the romantic fatalism that the Servant must avoid at all times, but it does catch the spirit of the Servant's myth and it is how he should appear in public. Fortune will play a large part in events, because it is beyond the capacity of men to control them. The Servant will study all the patterns of the lives and events that surround him and slowly place these patterns together. He acquires what romantic men call instinct. Although his actions are based on experience, he acts with the style of the romantic.

Machiavelli asserts that success follows those who are in accord with the spirit of the times. The Prince does not need to be in accord with the spirit of the times. He is the spirit of the times. By inspiring the Idea, the Prince will change fashion and that will become the expression of the spirit of the times.

Machiavelli, wondering how a Prince can rule well for a number of years and then fail, offers a number of causes. One he does not mention is the death wish in politics. Curiously, the Prince will be more likely to be subject to this death wish than lesser leaders. Although the tension involved in being a ruler is great, the tension of being *the* Prince is colossal. There may come times when the Prince will plot against himself as a means of deserting the Idea. Rulers will commonly train successors as a means of showing that they are not indispensable, and then dispense with them. This is not a sensible course of action, because it is a certain way of making enemies and because it gives credibility to these men which perhaps they do not deserve, having yet to prove themselves.*

If the Idea is strong enough, it will survive the departure of a Prince, but only if it is handed to those who truly deserve it. A man who pretends to believe in the Idea but would use it only to gain power and then throw it on one side will gain nothing that is worth having. Such a man lives always with the necessity of pleasing this one or that one—he is a name in history, one on a list of names, but a figure of little consequence, famous perhaps only for how long he has ruled, not for how he held office. Not a Prince, not even a person, only a man of commerce without an idea.†

The Servant must help the Prince to bear the burden of his situation, the claustrophobia and the inevitability of his continued rule. In these circumstances, the Servant must see that the Prince never actually appoints a successor, and if he does, the Servant appreciates that he must be dispensed with in a way that

---

* *Editor:* This was certainly the case when Margaret Thatcher used to promote the idea that John Major might succeed her as Prime Minister of Britain.
† *Editor:* This certainly turned out to be the case with Thatcher successor John Major.

causes no trouble. When the Prince entertains a death wish, the Servant must provide diversions. The greater the Idea, the more difficult to carry out, the harder it is to bear. There is an argument that life is short and that therefore events should be lived for the day. For the Prince and his Servant, life is very long. Events move very slowly, and each day must be treated as if it were a lifetime. It is this extended time that will set off the death wish in the Prince. Being intelligent, he will suffer from the fear of never-ending life. There is no cure for this other than to direct the Prince's energies towards strengthening the Idea. In adversity, the competent seek to expand, the incompetent try to cut back. The Prince must extend the scope of his Idea when times are hard. He has no alternative, for if he is to reduce his Idea, this will weaken it, and if the Idea is weakened all will be lost. Many will try to persaude the Prince to trim his Idea. They must never be allowed to succeed.

The Prince will come under pressure through the fear of his supporters. When the Prince has ruled for a long time, his supporters will doubt his ability to retain power and the Prince, hearing their words, will doubt his own ability. Being tired and facing these doubters, many of whom he himself has placed in their positions, he will feel lonely. This loneliness is the danger for the Prince, for it is a kind of pain felt only by successful Princes, and only after many years.

Those who will doubt the Prince's ability to retain power most are those who claim to be his strongest supporters. His enemies respect the Prince's ability to retain power, for they have tried and failed to displace him. A successful Prince can only be displaced by his own, for only they can believe that they do the Prince a favour. The Prince, knowing them to be his friends and feeling the pain of loneliness, may let them have their way. The Servant believes them to be traitors. How can this situation be avoided? The Servant can do very little except try to see that the Prince never suffers from loneliness.

A most dangerous breed are the men who think they want power, know how to obtain it, and, when it is theirs, give it away. This trait many people might believe to be uncommon. The reverse, however, is true in the circles where the Servant moves, and it leaves the Prince in grave danger if a man like this is working closely with the Prince. This trait is another variety of the death wish. It has been said that these men are lazy, keener on the chase than the kill. It is possible that they need to acquire the power simply for the intellectual satisfaction it gives—for the personal pride rather than the public pride. All they need to know is that power can be theirs; then they give it away. This is one of life's greatest conceits. It shows a kind of mental arrogance and, perhaps, a fear of not being able to hold on to power and of having it taken away. Although they do not seem to mind the mental humiliation of giving power away, this is in fact a form of controlled masochism. These men are very unreliable and the Servant must be alert to the first signs of this phenomenon. This is not failure, for these men do as they wish.

Machiavelli talks of failure, which is not a subject that absorbs us because this is not a handbook for the inadequate, but an argument that the Prince fully in possession of his Idea will succeed. This book has attempted to show how the Servant can help in this aim. Machiavelli talks of Princes reigning by the use of skill. Here we are talking about a Prince reigning through the strength of the Idea. The Servant's skill makes this possible, but the Idea will transcend the rule of Princes and the practice of Servants, until at last it is weakened by being diluted with the thoughts of others. It becomes cluttered by the parafanatics, and weakened further by their laziness. After the Prince and the Servant have gone, then only the very strongest Idea will survive, and only if it is taken up by another who may become a Prince. Thus the Prince must, in time, give thought to an heir.

There will come a time in the life of all Servants when the Prince has held power for many years and when the Idea of the Prince will be passing through a period of disrepute. Rivals will be gathering their strength to challenge the Prince. Many of the Prince's erstwhile supporters will have left the Prince's councils and some secretly and some publicly will harbour resentment towards him. Many of the Prince's current supporters will wonder how much longer the Prince can last. The Prince's enemies will attack the Prince's Idea, and his supporters will have doubts and wonder whether the Idea should be made more palatable to the people. This changing of the Idea is unacceptable to the Prince and to the Servant, for the Idea cannot be changed for political convenience. The current supporters of the Prince are worried about this, for they believe that the Prince has only a past and that they must secure their future. The leaders to whom these men might be drawn are men of convenience, none of them having a real Idea, none of them having a real body of support.

So the Prince believes that he is secure and, indeed, he is secure, for the majority of these groups support the Prince in preference to any one of the others who would be rulers. But fellow travellers of the Prince who call themselves supporters talk among themselves and do not always report the truth of their discussions. Out of these discussions will come rumours that the Prince is going to be overthrown by one of the rivals of the fellow travellers. And so his source of security, the split loyalties of the past, becomes the Prince's very danger. These fellow travellers will combine against one of their number who seems likely to defeat the Prince, and seek a new champion. In the end the Prince will have to throw the weight of his small band of loyal supporters behind one of the contestants who seems to support the Idea. His only option is to overcome those who had previously tried to overcome him, and so preserve the hope of a future for his Idea.★

There will be confusion and plotting among men who pledge their loyalty lightly, and self-interest will prevail. The Prince will be defeated and the new leader will proclaim the Idea, adjusted for convenience; but he does not have the Idea, nor is he, without the Idea, the Prince. It is the role of the Servant to prevent these events. When these events happen it is the beginning of the end for the Idea, and when the Idea begins to weaken it is finished, and no use at all to the people.

The true Servant must never offer to resign. The Prince cannot possibly accept his resignation. The Servant must not test his relationship with the Prince, for a Prince with whom he might do so is not worth the title. The Servant, if he believes the circumstances important, must organize his dismissal. Only he can judge if and when the Prince could be better served. Neither the courtiers, nor the people, nor even the Prince can judge the moment.

In times of extreme trouble, the populace and the Prince's supporters may look for a sacrifice. By tradition, the sacrifice is the Prince himself, but since the Prince must survive, the Servant will give the crowd a substitute: he must sacrifice himself. But the crowd is unlikely to be satisfied with a Servant, so he must arrange that the Prince clothe him in honour and speak of him as a Prince. The Servant must wear the robes of a Prince, look like a Prince and, for the first time, behave like one. Only then should he be sacrificed. And then only, the Servant can cast himself into the hands of the crowd. He must not ask the Prince

---

★ *Editor:* This refers to Margaret Thatcher's support of John Major.

to carry out this deed. It must be carried out properly in every respect. No hesitation, no half measures, for saving the Prince to carry on the Idea is the ultimate purpose of the Servant. It is an end that gives him true nobility.

In contemplating this act, the Servant must ask himself whether he has an alternative. Has he taken all known human emotions into account? Is he still sure that there is no choice? Has he taken into account the possibility of the unexpected? Only when he has thought about these matters thoroughly can he make this decision. Sacrificing the Servant will come as a complete surprise to the enemies of the Prince. They cannot expect this, for it was neither in the Prince's character, nor in his mind. It is the idea and action of the Servant. The only independent action that the Servant ever takes.

The surprise (the more so because the Prince, having heaped rewards on the Servant, will have increased dislike of him by both enemy and friend, thus making his sacrifice more effective) will give a great advantage to this Prince, allowing him to make a tactical retreat, regroup his Idea, engage a new Servant, and transform this unexpected turn of events into a lasting victory.

The Servant requires courage, loyalty and passion. He should always adopt the heroic position, for in defeat he will find the greatest victory.

EPILOGUE

Eventually there is a time for change, and when it comes, it will sweep far and wide. All our boundaries have changed, all the values that we believed true in the past seem worthless. Sent into the wilderness, the Prince will be reviled. But let the Servant take heart. Let him watch every moment of this change, for in time it will come again and his heroes will become the icons of the future. His Prince will again become the Prince, and his Idea will be restored.

The Servant must consider carefully how to conduct the affairs of the Prince in this empty time. He must consider whether he truly believes in the Idea and the Prince. If not, he should leave politics and take up agriculture. If he believes, the Servant must stay and serve the Prince and the Idea. No other Prince, however attractive, or, for that matter, however successful, is of any use to the Servant. The Servant must wait and arrange the affairs of the Prince, always keeping the Prince and the Idea pure and in readiness, for who can tell how the affairs of men may change again? The Servant must remember that the memories of men are very short and, after an interval, a useful Servant can recall the events that suit the Prince, and the population will remember them with joy, forgetting all else. These memories can form the base for the return of the Prince and his Idea. In fact, of course, Princes seldom return. More often, they return as the patrons of their Idea, using their Idea to shape events during their lives and readying their Idea to live long after them.

The Art of War

~

SUN TZU

[ONE]
LAYING PLANS

The art of war is of vital importance to the state. It is a matter of life and death, a road either to safety or to ruin. Hence it is a subject of inquiry which can on no account be neglected.

The art of war is governed by five constant factors, to be taken into account in one's deliberations, when seeking to determine the conditions obtaining in the field.

These are: the Moral Law, Heaven, Earth, the Commander, and Method and Discipline.

The Moral Law causes the people to be in complete accord with their ruler, so that they will follow him regardless of their lives, undismayed by any danger.

Heaven signifies night and day, cold and heat, times and seasons.

Earth comprises distances, great and small; danger and security; open ground and narrow passes; the chances of life and death.

The Commander stands for the virtues of wisdom, sincerity, benevolence, courage and strictness.

By *Method and Discipline* are to be understood the marshaling of the army in its proper subdivisions, the gradations of rank among the officers, the maintenance of roads by which supplies may reach the army, and the control of military expenditure.

These five heads should be familiar to every general. He who knows them will be victorious; he who knows them not will fail.

Therefore, in your deliberations, when seeking to determine the military conditions, let them be made the basis of a comparison, in this wise:

(1) Which of two sovereigns is imbued with the moral law?

(2) Which of two generals has most ability?

(3) With whom lie the advantages derived from heaven and earth?

(4) On which side is discipline most rigorously enforced?

(5) Which army is the stronger?

(6) On which side are officers and men most highly trained?

(7) In which army is there the greater constancy both in reward and punishment?

By means of these seven considerations I can forecast victory or defeat.

The general who harkens to my counsel and acts upon it, will conquer. Let such a one be retained in command! The general who harkens not to my counsel nor acts upon it, will suffer defeat. Let such a one be dismissed! While heeding the profit of my counsel, avail yourself also of any helpful circumstances over and beyond the ordinary rules. According as circumstances are favorable, one should modify one's plans.

All warfare is based on deception. Hence, when able to attack, we must seem unable; when using our forces, we must seem inactive; when we are near, we must make the enemy believe that we are away; when far away, we must make him believe we are near. Hold out baits to entice the enemy. Feign disorder, and crush him.

If he is secure at all points, be prepared for him. If he is superior in strength, evade him. If your opponent is of choleric temper, seek to irritate him. Pretend to be weak, that he may grow arrogant.

If he is inactive, give him no rest. If his forces are united, separate them. Attack him where he is unprepared, appear where you are not expected. These military devices, leading to victory, must not be divulged beforehand.

The general who wins a battle makes many calculations in his temple ere the battle is fought. The general who loses a battle makes but few calculations beforehand. Thus do many calculations lead to victory, and few calculations to defeat: How much more do no calculation at all pave the way to defeat! It is by attention to this point that I can see who is likely to win or lose.

[TWO]
WAGING WAR

In the operations of war, where there are in the field a thousand swift chariots, as many heavy chariots and a hundred thousand mail-clad soldiers, with provisions enough to carry them a thousand *li* [2.78 modern li make one mile] the expenditure at home and at the front, including entertainment of guests, small items such as glue and paint, and sums spent on chariots and armour, will reach the total of a thousand ounces of silver per day. Such is the cost of raising any army of 100,000 men.

When you engage in actual fighting, if victory is long in coming, the men's weapons will grow dull and their ardour will be damped. If you lay siege to a town, you will exhaust your strength. Again, if the campaign is protracted, the resources of the state will not be equal to the strain.

Now, when your weapons are dulled, your ardour damped, your strength exhausted and your treasure spent, other chieftains will spring up to take advantage of your extremity. Then no man, however wise, will rarely be able to avert the consequences that must ensue.

Thus, though we have heard of stupid haste in war, cleverness has never been associated with long delays. There is no instance of a country having been benefited from prolonged warfare.

It is only one who is thoroughly acquainted with the evils of war who can thoroughly understand the profitable way of carrying it on. The skillful soldier does not raise a second levy, neither are his supply-wagons loaded more than twice. Bring war material with you from home, but forage on the enemy. Thus the army will have enough for its needs.

Poverty of the state exchequer causes an army to be maintained by contributions from a distance. Contributing to maintain an army at a distance causes people to be impoverished.

On the other hand, the proximity of an army causes prices to go up; and high prices cause the people's substance to be drained away.

When their substance is drained away, the peasantry will be afflicted by heavy exactions.

With this loss of subsistence and exhaustion of strength, the homes of the people will be stripped bare and three-tenths of their incomes will be dissipated;* while government expenses for broken chariots, worn-out horses, breast-plates and helmets, bows and arrows, spears and shields, protective mantlets, draught-oxen and heavy wagons, will amount to four-tenths of its total revenue.

Hence a wise general makes a point of foraging on the enemy. One cartload of the enemy's provisions is equivalent to twenty of one's own, and likewise a single picul [about 133 pounds] of his provender is equivalent to twenty from one's own store.

In order to kill the enemy, men must be roused to anger; that there may be advantage from defeating the enemy, they must have their rewards.

Therefore in chariot fighting, when ten or more chariots have been taken, those should be rewarded who took the first. Our own flags should be substituted for those of the enemy, and the chariots mingled and used in conjunction with ours. The captured soldiers should be kindly treated and kept. This is called, using the conquered foe to augment one's own strength.

In war, then, let your great object be victory, not lengthy campaigns.

Thus is may be known that the leader of armies is the arbiter of the people's fate, the man on whom depends whether the nation shall be in peace or peril.

---

* *Editor:* Throughout this work, Sun Tzu is specific when he mentions degrees to which something or other affects a situation. These figures should not be taken literally despite the certainty with which Sun Tzu delivers them.

[THREE]
ATTACK BY STRATAGEM

In the practical art of war, the best thing of all is to take the enemy's country whole and intact; to shatter and destroy it is not so profitable. So, too, it is better to capture an army entire than to destroy it, to capture a regiment, a detachment or a company entire than to annihilate them.

Hence to fight and conquer in all your battles is not supreme excellence; supreme excellence consists in breaking the enemy's resistance without fighting.

Thus the highest form of generalship is to balk the enemy's plans. The next best is to prevent the junction of the enemy's forces. The next in order is to attack the enemy's army in the field. The worst policy of all is to besiege walled cities.

The rule is, not to besiege walled cities if it can possibly be avoided. The preparation of mantlets, movable shelters, and various implements of war, will take up three whole months; and the piling up of mounds [from which to attack] over against the walls will take three months more.

The general who is unable to control his impatience will launch his men to the assault like swarming ants, with the result that one-third of his men are slain, while the town remains untaken. Such are liable to be the disastrous effects of a siege.

Therefore the skillful leader subdues the enemy's troops without any fighting; he captures their cities without laying siege to them; he overthrows their kingdom without lengthy operations in the field.

With his forces intact he will dispute the mastery of the empire, and thus, without losing a man, his triumph will be complete. This is the method of attacking by stratagem.

It is the rule in war, if our forces are ten to the enemy's one, to surround him; if five to one, to attack him; if twice as numerous, to divide our army into two.

If equally matched, we can offer battle; if slightly inferior in numbers, we can avoid the enemy; if quite unequal in every way, we can flee from him. Hence, though an obstinate fight may be made by a small force, in the end it must be captured by the larger force.

Now the general is the bulwark of the state: if the bulwark is complete at all points, the state will be strong; if the bulwark is defective, the state will be weak.

There are three ways in which a ruler can bring misfortune upon his army:

By commanding the army to advance or to retreat, being ignorant of the fact that it cannot obey. This amounts to hobbling the army.

By attempting to govern an army in the same way as he administers a kingdom, being ignorant of the conditions which obtain in an army. This causes restlessness among the soldiers.

By employing the officers of his army without discrimination, through ignorance of the military principle of adapting action to circumstances. This shakes the confidence of the soldiers.

But when the army is restless and distrustful, trouble is sure to come from other feudal princes. This is simply equivalent in results to bringing anarchy into the army and flinging victory away.

Thus we may know that there are five essentials for victory:

He will win who knows when to fight and when not to fight.

He will win who knows how to handle both superior and inferior forces.

He will win whose army is animated by the same spirit throughout all ranks.

He will win who, prepared himself, waits to take the enemy unprepared.

He will win who has military capacity and is not interfered with by the sovereign.

Victory lies in the knowledge of those five points.

Hence the saying: If you know the enemy and know yourself, you need not fear the result of a hundred battles. If you know yourself, but not the enemy, for every victory gained you will also suffer a defeat. If you know neither the enemy nor yourself, you will succumb in every battle.

[FOUR]
TACTICAL DISPOSITIONS

The good fighters of old first put themselves beyond the possibility of defeat and then waited for an opportunity of defeating the enemy.

To secure ourselves against defeat lies in our own hands, but the opportunity of defeating the enemy is provided by the enemy himself.

Thus the good fighter is able to secure himself against defeat, but cannot make certain of defeating the enemy.

Hence the saying: One may *know* how to conquer without being able to do it.

Security against defeat implies defensive tactics; ability to defeat the enemy means taking the offensive.

Standing on the defensive indicates insufficient strength; attacking, a superabundance of strength.

The general who is skilled in defense, in effect, hides in the most secret recesses of the earth; he who is skilled in attack flashes forth from the topmost heights of heaven. Thus on the one hand we have ability to protect ourselves; on the other, a victory that is complete.

To see victory only when it is within the ken of the common herd is not the acme of excellence. Neither is it the acme of excellence if you conquer and the whole empire says, "Well done!"

To lift an autumn leaf is no sign of great strength; to see sun and moon is no sign of sharp sight; to hear the noise of thunder is no sign of a quick ear. What the ancients called a clever fighter is one who not only wins, but excels in winning with ease.

Hence his victories bring him neither reputation for wisdom nor credit for courage. He wins his battles by making no mistakes. Avoidance of mistakes establishes the certainty of victory, for it means conquering an enemy that is already defeated.

Hence the skillful fighter puts himself into a position which makes defeat impossible, and does not miss the moment for defeating the enemy.

Thus it is that in war the victorious strategist seeks battle after his plans indicate that victory is possible under them, whereas he who is destined to defeat first fights without skillful planning and expects victory to come without planning.

The consummate leader cultivates the moral law, and strictly adheres to method and discipline. Thus it is in his power to control success.

In respect of military method, we have: First, measurement; second, estimation of quantity; third, calculation; fourth, balancing of chances; fifth, victory.

Measurement owes its existence to earth; estimation of quantity to measurement; calculation to estimation of quantity; balancing of chances to calculation; and victory to balancing of chances.

A victorious army opposed to a routed one, is as a pound's weight placed in the scale against a single grain. The onrush of a conquering force is like the bursting of pent-up waters into a chasm a thousand fathoms deep. So much for tactical dispositions.

[FIVE]
USE OF ENERGY

The control of a large force is the same in principle as the control of a few men. It is merely a question of dividing up their numbers.

Fighting with a large army under your command is nowise different from fighting with a small one. It is merely a question of instituting signs and signals.

To ensure that your whole host may withstand the brunt of the enemy's attack and remain unshaken is effected by direct and indirect maneuvers.

That the impact of your army may be like a grindstone dashed against an egg. That is effected by the science involving contacts between weak points and strong.

In all fighting, the direct method may be used for joining battle, but indirect methods will be needed in order to ensure victory.

Indirect tactics, efficiently applied, are inexhaustible as heaven and earth, unending as the flow of rivers and streams; like the sun and moon, they end their course but to begin anew; like the four seasons, they pass to return once more.

There are not more than five musical notes* yet the combinations of these five give rise to more melodies than probably can ever be heard.† There are not more than three primary colors, yet in combination they produce more hues than can ever be seen.‡ There are not more than five tastes [sour, acrid, salt, sweet, bitter], yet combinations of them yield more flavors than can ever be tasted.

In battle, there are not more than two methods of attack— the direct and indirect; yet these two in combination give rise to an endless series of maneuvers. The direct and indirect lead on to each other in turn. It is like moving in a circle—you never come to an end. Who can exhaust the possibilities of their combination?

---

* *Editor:* Only five musical notes were used in the music of Sun Tzu's China.
† *Editor:* This is not totally true.
‡ *Editor:* On the other hand, this is true. Sun Tzu clearly knew more about painting than music and more about people than either of these arts.

The onset of troops is like the rush of a torrent which will even roll stones along its course.

The quality of decision is like the well-timed swoop of a falcon which enables it to strike and destroy its victim.

Therefore the good fighter will be terrible in his onset, and prompt in his decision.

Energy may be likened to the bending of a cross-bow; decision, to the releasing of the trigger.

Amid the turmoil and tumult of battle, there may be seeming disorder and yet no real disorder at all. Amid confusion and chaos, your array may be without apparent head or tail, yet it will be proof against defeat.

Simulated disorder postulates perfect discipline; simulated fear postulates courage; simulated weakness postulates strength.

Hiding order beneath the cloak of disorder is simply a question of subdivision; concealing courage under a show of timidity presupposes a fund of latent energy; masking strength with weakness is to be effected by tactical dispositions.

Thus one who is skillful at keeping the enemy on the move maintains deceitful appearances, according to which the enemy will act.

By holding out baits, he keeps him on the march; then with a body of picked men he lies in wait for him.

The clever combatant looks to the effect of combined energy, and does not require too much from individuals. Hence his ability to pick out the right men and to utilize combined energy.

utilizes combined energy, his fighting men be-
e like unto rolling logs or stones. For it is the na-
r stone to remain motionless on level ground, and
n on a slope; if four cornered, to come to a stand-
und-shaped to go rolling down.

e energy developed by good fighting men is as the
of a round stone rolled down a mountain thousands
eight. So much on the subject of energy.

[SIX]
WEAK POINTS AND STRONG

Whoever is first in the field and awaits the coming of the enemy, will be fresh for the fight; whoever is second in the field and has to hasten to the battle, will arrive exhausted.

Therefore the clever combatant imposes his will on the enemy, but does not allow the enemy's will to be imposed on him.

By holding out advantages to him he can cause the enemy to approach of his own accord; or by inflicting damage he can make it impossible for the enemy to draw near.

If the enemy is taking his ease he can harass him; if well supplied he can starve him out; if quietly encamped, he can force him to move.

Appear at points which the enemy must hasten to defend; march swiftly to places where you are not expected.

An army may march great distances without distress if it marches through country where the enemy is not.

You can be sure of succeeding in your attacks if
places which are not defended. You can insure the safet
defense if you hold only positions that cannot be attacke

Hence the general is skillful in attack whose opponent
not know what to defend; and he is skillful in defense wi
opponent does not know what to attack.

O divine art of subtlety and secrecy! Through you we learn
to be invisible, through you inaudible; and hence hold the
enemy's fate in our hands.

You may advance and be absolutely irresistible if you make for
the enemy's weak points; you may retire and be safe from pursuit
if your movements are more rapid than those of the enemy.

If we wish to fight the enemy can be forced to an engagement even though he be sheltered behind a high rampart and a
deep ditch. All we need to do is to attack some other place
which he will be obliged to relieve.

If we do not wish to fight, we can prevent the enemy from
engaging us even though the lines of our encampment be merely
traced on the ground. All we need to do is to throw something
unused and unaccountable in his way.

By discovering the enemy's dispositions and remaining invisible ourselves, we can keep our forces concentrated while the
enemy must be divided.

We can form a single united body, while the enemy must
split up into fractions. Hence there will be a whole pitted
against separate parts of a whole, which means that we shall be
many in collected mass to the enemy's separate few, amongst his
separated parts.

And if we are thus able to attack an inferior force with a superior one, our opponents will be in dire straits.

The spot where we intend to fight must not be made known; for then the enemy will have to prepare against a possible attack at several different points; and his forces being thus distributed in many directions, the numbers we shall have to face at any given point will be proportionately few.

For should the enemy strengthen his van, he will weaken his rear; should he strengthen his rear, he will weaken his van; should he strengthen his left, he will weaken his right; should he strengthen his right, he will weaken his left. If he sends reinforcements everywhere, he will be everywhere weak.

Numerical weakness comes from having to prepare against possible attacks; numerical strength, from compelling our adversary to make these preparations against us.

Knowing the place and time of the coming battle, we may concentrate from great distances in order to fight.

But if neither time nor place be known, then the left wing will be impotent to succor the right, the right equally impotent to succor the left, the van unable to relieve the rear, or the rear to support the van. How much more so if the furthest portions of the army are anything under a hundred *li* apart, and even the nearest are separated by several *li*.

Though according to my estimate the soldiers of Yüeh exceed our own in number, that shall advantage them nothing in the matter of victory. I say then that victory can be achieved.

Though the enemy be stronger in numbers, we may prevent him from fighting. Scheme so as to discover his plans and the likelihood of their success.

Rouse him, and learn the principle of his activity or inactivity. Force him to reveal himself, so as to find out his vulnerable spots.

Carefully compare the opposing army with our own, so that you may know where strength is superabundant and where it is deficient.

In making tactical dispositions, the highest pitch you can attain is to conceal them; conceal your dispositions and you will be safe from the prying of the subtlest of spies, from the machinations of the wisest brains.

How victory may be produced by this from the enemy's own tactics is what the multitude cannot comprehend.

All men can see these tactics whereby I conquer, but what none can see is the strategy out of which victory is evolved.

Do not repeat the tactics which have gained you one victory, but let your methods be regulated by the infinite variety of circumstances.

Military tactics are like unto water, for water in its natural course runs away from high places and hastens downwards. So in war, the way to avoid what is strong is to strike what is weak.

Water shapes its course according to the ground over which it flows; the soldier works out his victory in relation to the foe whom he is facing.

Therefore, just as water retains no constant shape, so in warfare there are no constant conditions.

He who can modify his tactics in relation to his opponent and thereby succeed in winning, may be called a heaven-born captain.

The five elements [water, fire, wood, metal, earth] are not always equally prominent; the four seasons make way for each other in turn. There are short days and long; the moon has its periods of waning and waxing.

[SEVEN]
MANEUVERING AN ARMY

In war, the general receives his commands from the sovereign. Having collected an army and concentrated his forces, he he must blend and harmonize the different element thereof before pitching his camp.

After that, comes tactical maneuvering, than which there is nothing more difficult. The difficulty of tactical maneuvering consists in turning the devious into the direct and misfortune into gain.

Thus, to take a long circuitous route, after enticing the enemy out of the way, and though starting after him to contrive to reach the goal before him, shows knowledge of the artifice of deviation.

Maneuvering with an army is advantageous; with an undisciplined multitude, most dangerous.

If you set a fully equipped army in march in order to snatch an advantage, the chances are that you will be too late. On the other hand, to detach a flying column for the purpose involves the sacrifice of its baggage and stores.

Thus, if you order your men to make forced marches without halting day or night, covering double the usual distance at a stretch, and doing a hundred *li* in order to wrest an advantage, the leaders of your three divisions will fall into the hands of the enemy.

The stronger men will be in front, the jaded ones will fall behind, and by this only one-tenth of your army will reach its destination.

If you march fifty *li* in order to outmaneuver the enemy, you will lose the leader of your first division, and only half your force will reach its goal.

If you march thirty *li* with the same object, two-thirds of your army will arrive.

We may take it then that an army without its baggage train is lost; without provisions it is lost; without bases of supply it is lost.

We cannot enter into alliances until we are acquainted with the designs of our neighbors.

We are not fit to lead an army on the march unless we are familiar with the face of the country—its mountains and forests, its pitfalls.

We shall be unable to turn natural advantages to account unless we make use of local guides.

In war, practice dissimulation, and you will succeed. Move only if there is a real advantage to be gained.

Whether to concentrate or to divide your troops must be decided by circumstances.

Let your rapidity be that of the wind, your compactness that of the forest. In raiding and plundering be like fire, in immovability like a mountain.

Keep your plans dark and impenetrable as night and when you move, fall like a thunderbolt.

When you plunder a countryside, let the spoil be divided amongst your men; when you capture new territory, cut it up into allotments for the benefit of the soldiery.

Ponder and deliberate before you make a move.

He will conquer who has learnt the artifice of deviation. Such is the art of maneuvering.

The *Book of Army Management* [an unknown book] says: On the field of battle the spoken word does not carry far enough: hence the institution of gongs and drums. Nor can ordinary objects be seen clearly enough; hence the institution of banners and flags.

Gongs and drums, banners and flags are means whereby the ears and eyes of the host may be focussed on one particular point.

The host thus forming a single united body, it is impossible either for the brave to advance alone, or for the cowardly to retreat alone. This is the art of handling large masses of men.

In night-fighting, then, make much use of signal fires and drums, and in fighting by day of flags and banners as a means of guiding your men through their ears and eyes.

A whole army may be robbed of its spirit; a commander-in-chief may be robbed of his presence of mind.

Now a soldier's spirit is keenest in the morning; by noonday it has begun to flag and in the evening his mind is bent only on returning to camp.

A clever general, therefore, avoids an army when its spirit is keen, but attacks it when it is sluggish and inclined to retreat. This is the art of studying moods.

Disciplined and calm, to await the appearance of disorder and hubbub amongst the enemy—this is the art of retaining self possession.

To be near the goal while the enemy is still far from it, to wait at ease while the enemy is toiling and struggling, to be well fed while the enemy is famished—this is the art of husbanding one's strength.

To refrain from intercepting an enemy whose ranks are in perfect order, to refrain from attacking an army drawn up in calm and confident array—this is the art of studying circumstances.

It is a military axiom not to advance uphill against the enemy, nor to oppose him when he comes downhill.

Do not pursue an enemy who simulates flight; do not attack soldiers whose temper is keen.

Do not swallow a bait offered by the enemy. Do not interfere with an army that is retreating into its own territory.

When you surround an army leave an outlet free. Do not press a desperate foe too hard.

Such is the art of warfare.

[EIGHT]
VARIATION OF TACTICS

In war, the general receives his commands from the sovereign, collects his army and concentrates his forces.

When in difficult country do not encamp. In country where high roads intersect join hands with your allies. Do not linger in dangerously isolated positions. In hemmed-in situations where you are you must resort to stratagem. In a desperate position, you must fight.

There are roads which must not be followed, armies which must not be attacked, towns which must not be besieged, positions which must not be contested, commands of the sovereign which must not be obeyed.

The general who thoroughly understands the advantages that accompany variation of tactics knows how to handle his troops.

The general who does not understand these may be well acquainted with the configuration of the country, yet he will not be able to turn his knowledge to practical account.

The student of war who is unversed in the art of varying his plans, even though he be acquainted with the Five Advantages will fail to make the best use of his men.

Hence in the wise leader's plans, considerations of advantage will be blended. If our expectation of advantage be tempered in this way, we may succeed in accomplishing the essential part of our schemes.

If, on the other hand, in the midst of difficulties we are always ready to seize an advantage, we may extricate ourselves from misfortune.

Reduce hostile chiefs by inflicting damage on them; make trouble for them, and keep them constantly engaged; hold out specious allurements, and make them rush to any given point.

The art of war teaches us to rely not on the likelihood of the enemy not coming, but on our own readiness to receive him; not on the chance of his not attacking, but rather on the fact that we have made our position unassailable.

There are five dangerous faults which may affect a general: Recklessness, which leads to destruction; cowardice, which leads to capture; a hasty temper that can be provoked by insults; a delicacy of honor that is sensitive to shame; over-solicitude for his men, which exposes him to worry and trouble. These are the five besetting sins of a general, ruinous to the conduct of war.

When an army is overthrown and its leader slain, the cause will surely be found among the five dangerous faults. Let them be a subject of meditation.

[NINE]
THE ARMY ON THE MARCH

We now come to the question of encamping the army and observing signs of the enemy. Pass quickly over mountains [which are barren of fodder] and keep in the neighborhood of valleys.

Camp in high places. Do not climb heights in order to fight. So much for mountain warfare.

After crossing a river, you should get far away from it [in order to tempt the enemy to follow you across].

When an invading force crosses a river in its onward march, do not advance to meet it in midstream. It will be best to let the army get across and then deliver your attack.

If you are anxious to fight, you should not go to meet the invader near a river which he has to cross [for fear of preventing his crossing].

Moor your craft higher up than the enemy and facing the sun. Do not move upstream to meet the enemy. So much for river warfare.

In crossing marshes, your sole concern should be to get over them quickly, without any delay.

If forced to fight in a marsh, you should have the water and grass near you, and get your back to a clump of trees. So much for marshes.

In dry, level country, take up an easily accessible position with rising ground to your right and on your rear, so that the danger may be in front, and safety lie behind. So much for flat country.

These are the four useful branches of military knowledge which enabled the Yellow Emperor⋆ to vanquish four several sovereigns.

In battle and maneuvering all armies should prefer high ground to low and sunny places to dark. If you are careful of your men, and camp on hard ground, the army will be free from diseases, and this will spell victory.

When you come to a hill or a bank, occupy the sunny side, with the slope on your right rear. Thus you will at once act for the benefit of your soldiers and utilize the natural advantages of the ground.

When, in consequence of heavy rains up-country, a river which you wish to ford is swollen and flecked with foam, you must wait until it subsides. Country in which there are precipitous cliffs with torrents running between, deep natural hollows, confined places, tangled thickets, quagmires and crevasses, should be left with all possible speed and not even approached.

⋆ *Editor:* It is likely that this emperor was from the Chin dynasty (256–207 B.C.), from which the name "China" is derived.

While we keep away from such places, we should try to get the enemy to approach them; while we face them, we should let the enemy have them on his rear.

If in the neighborhood of your camp there should be hilly country, ponds surrounded by aquatic grass, hollow basins filled with reeds, or woods with thick undergrowth, they must be carefully searched; for these are places where men in ambush or spies are likely to be lurking.

When the enemy is close at hand and remains quiet, he is relying on the natural strength of his position.

When he keeps aloof and tries to provoke a battle, he is anxious for the other side to advance.

If his place of encampment is easy of access, he is tendering a bait.

Movement amongst the trees of a forest shows that the enemy is advancing. The appearance of a number of screens [to fake an ambush] in the midst of thick grass means that the enemy wants to make us suspicious.

The rising of birds in their flight is the sign of an ambuscade. Startled beasts indicate that a sudden attack is coming.

When there is dust rising in a high column, it is the sign of chariots advancing; when the dust is low, but spread over a wide area, it betokens the approach of infantry. When it branches out in different directions, it shows that parties have been sent out to collect firewood. A few clouds of dust moving to and fro signify that the army is camping.

Placatory words and increased preparations are signs that the enemy is about to advance. Violent language and driving forward as if to the attack may be signs that he will retreat.

When light chariots come out and take up a position on the wings, it is a sign that the enemy is forming for battle.

Peace proposals unaccompanied by a sworn covenant indicate a plot.

When there is much running about it means that the critical moment has come.

When some of the enemy are seen advancing and some retreating, it is a lure.

When soldiers stand leaning on their spears, they are faint from want of food.

If those who are sent to draw water begin by drinking themselves, the army is suffering from thirst.

If the enemy sees an advantage to be gained and makes no effort to secure it, the soldiers are exhausted.

If birds gather on any spot, it is unoccupied. Clamour by night betokens nervousness.

If there is disturbance in the camp [as indicated by observation, reports of spies or otherwise], the general's authority is weak. If the banners and flags are shifted about, sedition is afoot. If the officers are angry, the men are weary.

When an army feeds its horses with grain and kills its cattle for food, and when the men do not hang their cooking pots over the camp-fires, showing that they will not return to their tents, you may know that they are determined to fight to the death.

The sight of men whispering together in small knots and speaking in subdued tones points to dissatisfaction amongst the rank and file.

Too frequent rewards signify that the enemy is at the end of his resources [because, when an army is hard pressed there is always fear of mutiny and lavish rewards are given to keep the men happy]. Too many punishments betray a condition of dire distress [because in such conditions discipline is relaxed and unwonted severity is necessary to keep the men to their duty].

To begin by bluster, but afterwards to take fright at the enemy's numbers, shows supreme lack of intelligence.

When envoys are sent with compliments in their mouths, it is a sign that the enemy wishes for a truce.

If the enemy's troops march up angrily and remain facing yours for a long time without either joining battle or taking themselves off again, the situation is one that demands great vigilance and circumspection.

If our troops are no more in number than the enemy, that is amply sufficient; it means that no direct attack may be made. What we can do is simply to concentrate all our available strength, keep a close watch on the enemy, and obtain reinforcements.

He who exercises no forethought, but makes light of his opponents risks being captured by them.

If soldiers are punished before they have grown attached to you, they will not prove submissive; and unless submissive, they will be practically useless. If, when the soldiers have become attached to you, punishments are not enforced, they will still be useless.

Therefore soldiers must be treated in the first instance with humanity, but kept under control by iron discipline. This is one of the certain roads to victory.

If in training soldiers commands are habitually enforced, the army will be well disciplined.

If a general shows confidence in his men but always insists on his orders being obeyed, the gain will be mutual.

[TEN]
CLASSIFICATION OF TERRAIN

We may distinguish six kinds of terrain: Accessible ground, entangling ground, temporizing ground, narrow passes, precipitous heights and positions at a great distance from the enemy.

Accessible. Ground which can be freely traversed by both sides. With regard to ground of this nature, be before the enemy in occupying the raised and sunny spots, and carefully guard your line of supplies. Then you will be able to fight with advantage.

Entangling. Ground which can be abandoned but is hard to reoccupy. From a position of this sort, if the enemy is unprepared, you may sally forth and defeat him. But if the enemy is prepared for your coming, and you fail to defeat him, then, return being impossible, disaster will ensue.

Temporizing. Ground whereon the position is such that neither side will gain by making the first move. In a position of this sort, even though the enemy should offer us an attractive bait, it will be advisable not to stir forth, but rather to retreat, thus enticing the enemy in his turn; then, when part of his army has come out, we may deliver our attack with advantage.

Narrow passes. If you can occupy them first, let them be strongly garrisoned and await the advent of the enemy. Should the enemy forestall you in occupying a pass, do not go after him if the pass is fully garrisoned, but only if it is weakly garrisoned.

Heights. You should occupy raised and sunny spots, and there wait for him to come up. If the enemy has occupied them before you, do not follow him, but retreat to entice him away.

Positions. If you are situated at a great distance from the enemy, and the strength of the two armies is equal, it is not easy to provoke a battle, and fighting will be to your disadvantage.

These six are the principles of terrain. The general who holds a responsible post must study them.

An army is exposed to six several calamities not arising from natural causes, but from faults for which the general is responsible. These are: flight, insubordination, collapse, ruin, disorganization and rout.

Other conditions being equal, if one force is hurled against another ten times its size, the result will be the flight of the former.

When the common soldiers are too strong and their officers too weak, the result is insubordination. When the officers are too strong and the common soldiers too weak, the result is collapse.

When the higher officers are angry and insubordinate, and on meeting the enemy give battle independently, on their own account from a feeling of resentment, before the commander-in-chief can tell whether or not he is in a position to fight, the result is ruin.

When the general is weak and without authority; when his orders are not clear and distinct; when there are no fixed duties assigned to officers and men, and the ranks are formed in a slovenly haphazard manner, the result is utter disorganization.

When a general, unable to estimate the enemy's strength, allows an inferior force to engage a larger one, or hurls a weak detachment against a powerful one, and neglects to place picked soldiers in the front rank, the result must be a rout.

These are six ways of courting defeat, which must be carefully noted by the general in active command and service.

The natural formation of the country is the soldier's best ally; but a power of estimating the adversary, of controlling the forces of victory, and of shrewdly calculating difficulties, dangers and distances, constitutes the test of a great general.

He who knows these things, and in fighting puts his knowledge into practice, will win his battles. He who knows them not, will surely be defeated.

If fighting is reasonably sure to result in victory, then you must fight, even though the ruler forbid it; if fighting promises not to result in victory, then you must not fight, even at the ruler's bidding.

The general who advances without coveting fame and retreats without fearing disgrace, whose only thought is to protect his country and do good service for his sovereign, is the jewel of the kingdom.

Regard your soldiers as your children, and they will follow you wherever you may lead. Look on them as your own beloved sons, and they will stand by you even unto death.

If, however, you are indulgent, but unable to make your authority felt; kind-hearted, but unable to enforce your commands; and incapable, moreover, of quelling disorder, then your soldiers must be likened to spoiled children. They are useless for any practical purpose.

If we know that our own men are in a condition to attack, but are unaware that the enemy is not open to attack, we have gone only halfway towards victory.

If we know that the enemy is open to attack, but are unaware that our own men are not in a condition to attack, we have gone only halfway towards victory.

If we know that the enemy is open to attack, and also know that our own men are in a condition to attack, but are unaware that the nature of the ground makes fighting impracticable, we have gone only halfway towards victory.

Hence the experienced soldier, once in motion, is never bewildered. Once he has broken camp, he is never at a loss.

Hence the saying: If you know the enemy and know yourself, your victory will not stand in doubt; if you know Heaven and know Earth, you may make your victory complete.

[ELEVEN]

THE NINE SITUATIONS

The art of war recognizes nine varieties of ground: Dispersive ground, facile ground, contentious ground, open ground, ground of intersecting highways, serious ground, difficult ground, hemmed-in ground and desperate ground.

Dispersive. Ground whereon a chieftain is fighting in his own territory.

Facile. Ground whereon he has penetrated into hostile territory, but to no great distance, it is facile ground.

Contentious. Ground, the possession of which imports great advantage to either side.

Open. Ground on which each side has liberty of movement.

Intersecting highways. Ground which forms the key to three contiguous states, so that he who occupies it first has most of the Empire at his command.

Serious. Ground whereon an army has penetrated into the heart of a hostile country, leaving a number of fortified cities in his rear.

Difficult. Ground that includes mountain forests, rugged steeps, marshes and fens—all country that is hard to traverse.

Hemmed-in. Ground which is reached through narrow gorges and from which we can retire only by tortuous paths, so that a small number of the enemy would suffice to crush a large body of our men.

Desperate. Ground on which we can only be saved from destruction by fighting without delay.

On dispersive ground, therefore, fight not.

On facile ground, halt not.

On contentious ground, attack not.

On open ground, do not try to block the enemy's way.

On ground of intersecting highways, join hands with your allies.

On serious ground, gather in plunder.

On desperate ground, fight.

On hemmed-in ground, resort to stratagem.

Those who of old were called skillful leaders knew how to drive a wedge between the enemy's front and rear; to prevent co-operation between his large and small divisions; to hinder

the good troops from rescuing the bad, the officers from rally-
ing their men.

When the enemy's men were scattered, they prevented them
from concentrating; even when their forces were united, they
managed to keep them in disorder.

When it was to their advantage, they made a forward move;
when otherwise, they stopped still.

When asked how to cope with a great host of the enemy in
orderly array and on the point of marching to the attack, I
should say: "Begin by seizing something which your opponent
holds dear; then he will be amenable to your will."

Rapidity is the essence of war; take advantage of the enemy's
unreadiness, make your way by unexpected routes, and attack
unguarded spots.

The following are principles to be observed by an invading
force: the further you penetrate into a country, the greater will
be the solidarity of your troops, and thus the defenders will not
prevail against you.

Make forays in fertile country in order to supply your army
with food.

Carefully study the well-being of your men, and do not
overtax them. Concentrate your energy and hoard your strength.
Keep your army continually on the move and devise unfath-
omable plans.

Throw your soldiers into positions whence there is no escape, and they will prefer death to flight. Officers and men
alike will put forth their uttermost strength.

Soldiers when in desperate straits lose the sense of fear. If there is no place of refuge, they will stand firm. If they are in the heart of a hostile country, they will show a stubborn front. If there is no help for it, they will fight hard.

Thus, without waiting to be marshaled, the soldiers will be constantly on the *qui vive;* without waiting to be asked, they will do your will; without restrictions, they will be faithful; without giving orders, they can be trusted.

Prohibit seeking for omens, and do away with superstitious doubts. Then, until death comes, no apparently predestined calamity need be feared.

If our soldiers are not overburdened with money, it is not because they have a distaste for riches; if their lives are not unduly long, it is not because they are disinclined to longevity.

On the day they are ordered out to battle, your soldiers may weep, those sitting up bedewing their garments, and those lying down letting the tears run down their cheeks. But let them once be brought to bay, and they will display the courage of any of our heroes.

The skillful tactician may be likened to the *shuai-jan,* a snake that is found in the Ch'ang mountains. Strike at its head and you will be attacked by its tail; strike at its tail, and you will be attacked by its head; strike at its middle, and you will be attacked by head and tail both.

Asked if an army can be made to imitate the *shuai-jan,* I should answer, yes. For the men of Wu and the men of Yüeh are enemies; yet if they are crossing a river in the same boat and are caught by a storm, they will come to each other's assistance just as the left hand helps the right.

Hence it is not enough to put one's trust in the tethering of horses, and the burying of chariot wheels in the ground.

The principle on which to manage an army is to set up one standard of courage which all must reach. How to make the best of both strong and weak is a question involving the proper use of ground.

Thus the skillful general conducts his army just as though he were leading a single man, willy-nilly, by the hand.

It is the business of a general to be quiet and thus ensure secrecy; upright and just, and thus maintain order. He must be able to mystify his officers and men by false reports and appearances, and thus keep them in total ignorance.

By altering his arrangements and changing his plans, he keeps the enemy without definite knowledge of his movements. By shifting his camp and taking circuitous routes, he prevents the enemy from anticipating his purpose.

At the critical moment, the leader of an army should act like one who has climbed up a height and then kick away the ladder behind him. He carries his men deep into hostile territory before he shows his hand.

He burns his boats and breaks his cooking pots; like a shepherd driving a flock of sheep, he drives his men this way and that, and none knows whither he is going.

To muster his host and bring it into danger—this may be termed the business of the general.

The different measures suited to the nine varieties of ground; the expediency of aggressive or defensive tactics; and the fundamental laws of human nature, are things that must most certainly be studied.

When invading hostile territory the general principle is that penetrating deeply brings cohesion; penetrating only a short way means dispersion.

When you leave your own country behind and take your army across neighbouring territory, you find yourself on critical ground. When there are means of communication on all four sides, the ground is one of intersecting highways.

When you penetrate deeply into a country, it is serious ground. When you penetrate but a little way, it is facile ground.

When you have the enemy's strongholds on your rear, and narrow passes in front, it is hemmed-in ground. When there is no place of refuge at all, it is desperate ground.

Therefore, on dispersive ground, I should inspire my men with unity of purpose. On facile ground, I should see that there is close connection between all parts of my army.

On contentious ground, I should hurry up my rear.

On open ground, I should keep a vigilant eye on my defenses. On ground of intersecting highways, I should consolidate my alliances.

On serious ground, I should try to ensure a continuous stream of supplies.★

On difficult ground, I should keep pushing on along the road.

★ *Editor:* The true meaning of this sentence is unknown. Some sources believe that it refers to availability of supplies from foraging rather than by a system of transport.

On hemmed-in ground, I should block any way of retreat. On desperate ground, I should proclaim to my soldiers the hopelessness of saving their lives. For it is the soldier's disposition to offer an obstinate resistance when surrounded, to fight hard when he cannot help himself and to obey promptly when he has fallen into danger.

We cannot enter into alliance with neighbouring princes until we are acquainted with their designs. We are not fit to lead an army on the march unless we are familiar with the face of the country—its mountains and forests, its pitfalls and precipices, its marshes and swamps. We shall be unable to turn natural advantages to account unless we make use of local guides.★

To be ignorant of any one of the following principles does not befit a warlike prince.

When a warlike prince attacks a powerful state, his generalship shows itself in preventing the concentration of the enemy's forces. He overawes his opponents, and their allies are prevented from joining against him.

Hence he does not strive to ally himself with all and sundry, nor does he foster the power of other states. He carries out his own secret designs, keeping his antagonists in awe. Thus he is able to capture their cities and overthrow their kingdoms.

Bestow rewards without regard to rule, issue orders without regard to previous arrangements and you will be able to handle a whole army.

★ *Editor:* Along with Machiavelli, Sun Tzu goes in for a good deal of duplication. This repetition helps give emphasis to his points and power to the writing.

Confront your soldiers with the deed itself; never let them know your design. When the outlook is bright, bring it before their eyes; but tell them nothing when the situation is gloomy.

Place your army in deadly peril and it will survive; plunge it into desperate straits and it will come off in safety.

For it is precisely when a force has fallen into harm's way that it is capable of striking a blow for victory.

Success in warfare is gained by carefully accommodating ourselves to the enemy's purpose.

By persistently hanging on the enemy's flank, we shall succeed in the long run in killing the commander-in-chief. This is called ability to accomplish a thing by sheer cunning.

On the day that you assume your command, block the frontier passes, void the official passports and stop the passage of all emissaries.

Be stern in the council chamber, so that you may control the situation.

If the enemy leaves a door open, you must rush in.

Forestall your opponent by seizing what he holds dear, and subtly contrive to time his arrival on the ground.

Walk in the path defined by rule,★ and accommodate yourself to the enemy until you can fight a decisive battle.

At first, then, exhibit the coyness of a maiden, until the enemy gives you an opening; afterwards emulate the rapidity

---

★ *Editor:* Some translations show this line as "Discard hard and fast rules." This would seem to be more in keeping with Sun Tzu's ideas. It is, however, not an important part of the passage—the real sense comes in the next line and paragraph.

of a running hare, and it will be too late for the enemy to oppose you.

[TWELVE]
ATTACK BY FIRE

There are five ways of attacking with fire. The first is to burn soldiers in their camp; the second is to burn stores; the third is to burn baggage-trains; the fourth is to burn arsenals and magazines; the fifth is to hurl dropping fire amongst the enemy.

In order to carry out an attack with fire, we must have means available; the material for raising fire should always be kept in readiness.

There is a proper season for making attacks with fire, and special days for starting a conflagration.

The proper season is when the weather is very dry; the special days are those when the moon is in the constellations of the Sieve, the Wall, the Wing or the Cross-bar; for these are all days of rising wind.

In attacking with fire, one should be prepared to meet five possible developments:

When fire breaks out inside the enemy's camp, respond at once with an attack from without.

If there is an outbreak of fire, but the enemy's soldiers remain quiet, bide your time.

When the force of the flames has reached its height, follow it up with an attack, if that be practicable; if not stay where you are.

If it is possible to make an assault with fire from without, do not wait for it to break out within, but deliver your attack at the favorable moment.

When you start a fire, be to windward of it. Do not attack from the leeward.

A wind that rises in the daytime lasts long, but a night breeze soon fails.

In every army, the five developments connected with fire must be known, the movements of the stars calculated and watch kept for the proper days.

Hence those who use fire as an aid to the attack show intelligence; those who use water as an aid to the attack gain an accession of strength.

By means of water an enemy may be intercepted, but not robbed of all his belongings.

Unhappy is the fate of one who tries to win his battles and succeed in his attacks without cultivating the spirit of enterprise; for the result is waste of time and general stagnation.

Hence the saying: The enlightened ruler lays his plans well ahead; the good general cultivates his resources.

Move not unless you see an advantage; use not your troops unless there is something to be gained; fight not unless the position is critical.

No ruler should put troops into the field merely to gratify his own spleen; no general should fight a battle simply out of pique.

If it is to your advantage to make a forward move, make a forward move; if not, stay where you are.

Anger may in time change to gladness, vexation may be succeeded by content.

But a kingdom that has once been destroyed can never come again into being; nor can the dead ever be brought back to life.

Hence the enlightened ruler is heedful, and the good general full of caution. This is the way to keep a country at peace and an army intact.

[THIRTEEN]
USE OF SPIES

Raising a host of a hundred thousand men and marching them great distances entails heavy loss on the people and a drain on the resources of the state. The daily expenditure will amount to a thousand ounces of silver. There will be commotion at home and abroad, and men will drop down exhausted on the highways. As many as seven hundred thousand families will be impeded in their labor.

Hostile armies may face each other for years, striving for victory which is decided in a single day. This being so, to remain in ignorance of the enemy's condition simply because one grudges the outlay of a hundred ounces of silver in honours and emoluments, is the height of inhumanity.

One who acts thus is no leader of men, no present help to his sovereign, no master of victory.

Thus, what enables the wise sovereign and the good general to strike and conquer, and achieve things beyond the reach of ordinary men, is foreknowledge.

Now this foreknowledge cannot be elicited from spirits; it cannot be obtained inductively from experience, nor by any deductive calculation.

Knowledge of the enemy's dispositions can only be obtained from other men. Hence the use of spies, of whom there are five classes: Local, inward, converted, doomed and surviving spies.

When these five kinds of spy are all at work, none can discover all of the ramifications of your secret spy system. This is called "divine manipulation of the threads." It is the sovereign's most precious faculty.

Local spying, invaders employing the services of the inhabitants of a district.

Inward spies, making use of officials of the enemy.

Converted spies, getting hold of the enemy's spies and using them for our own purposes.

Doomed spies, doing certain things openly for purposes of deception, and allowing our own spies to know them and report them to the enemy.

Surviving spies, those who bring back news from the enemy's camp.

Hence it is that with none in the whole army are more intimate relations to be maintained than with spies. None should be more liberally rewarded. In no other business should greater secrecy be preserved. Spies cannot be usefully employed without certain intuitive sagacity.

They cannot be properly managed without benevolence and straightforwardness.

Without subtle ingenuity of mind, one cannot make certain of the truth of their reports. Be subtle, and use your spies for every kind of business.

If a secret piece of news is divulged by a spy before the time is ripe, he must be put to death together with the man to whom the secret was told.★

Whether the object be to crush an army, to storm a city, or to assassinate an individual, it is always necessary to begin by finding out the names of the attendants, the aides-de-camp, the doorkeepers and sentries of the general in command. Our spies must be commissioned to ascertain these.

The enemy's spies who have come to spy on us must be sought out, tempted with bribes, led away and comfortably housed. Thus they will become converted spies and available for our service.

It is through the information brought by the converted spy that we are able to acquire and employ local and inward spies.

It is owing to his information, again, that we can cause the doomed spy to carry false tidings to the enemy. [Because the converted spy knows how the enemy can best be deceived.]

Lastly, it is by his information that the surviving spy can be used on appointed occasions.

The end and aim of spying in all its five varieties is knowledge of the enemy; and this knowledge can only be derived, in the first instance, from the converted spy. Hence it is essential that the converted spy be treated with the utmost liberality.

Of old, the rise of the Yin dynasty [1766–1122 B.C.] was due to I Chih who had served under the Hsia [2205–1766 B.C.].

★ *Editor:* Sun Tzu was clearly a ruthless leader.

Likewise, the rise of the Chou dynasty [1122–256 B.C.] was due to Lü Ya who had served under the Yin.

Hence it is only the enlightened ruler and the wise general who will use the highest intelligence of the army for purposes of spying, and thereby they achieve great results. Spies are a most important element in war, because on them largely depends an army's ability to move.